Arnold Jacobs
The Legacy of a Master

The personal and pedagogical
recollections of thirty-one of his
colleagues, students, and friends.

Edited and Collected
by M. Dee Stewart

The Instrumentalist Publishing Company

i

TABLE OF CONTENTS

Notes to the Reader

Musicians rarely have the opportunity to appreciate the works of a great pedagogue. Teachers frequently theorize on their methods in books and articles, but the products of their teaching, the successful students, are often less obvious. In your hands rest the tangible results of one great teacher. This sampling of memoirs by Arnold Jacobs' students and colleagues is truly the *Legacy of a Master*.

Compiling this collection has been exciting and stimulating. A stimulus is defined as "something that rouses the mind and spirit" and I have certainly been roused by the dedication, devotion, and determination of those who have contributed to this project. Arnold Jacobs' profound influence on these people is evident. These glimpses of personal development, attitudes, and comments of contentment indicate that his influence has extended well beyond the musical sphere. Reliving my own musical development while reading and editing the words of 31 others has evoked endless speculation regarding the complex truths and simple applications of great teaching.

This project developed from discussions with many musicians who appreciate the Arnold Jacobs approach. Lack of documentation was the main source of concern. Indiana University was approached for funds, and eventually a small grant was given to cover some of the expenses. Several avenues for publication were considered, and as a result this book has been developed. A series of videotapes is also planned.

Drawing from casual conversations with Mr. Jacobs and others, a list of 50 names of students and colleagues was assembled. Initially, this group of musicians represented all the brass instruments and covered a period of 50 years. These people were contacted and 31 responded with completed articles and statements. This is a fine indication of the dedication to Arnold Jacobs by a group of people whose primary skill is not the written word. Priceless pictures, tapes, and other memorabilia were also received in substantial numbers.

Most of the contributors mentioned other fellow musicians whom they felt should be included. This list is certainly as impressive as the first and to those I express concern that they were not given this forum. The balance and number of the original list appeared to be appropriate, and the succeeding steps of the project needed to be addressed. As Mr. Jacobs stated over and over, "There are so many!"

It should be understood that this collection of contributions does not contain the words of Arnold Jacobs. However, there are many pedagogical insights and methods contained herein. No attempt was made to direct the thinking of the contributors and, as thoughts and phrases are repeated, a tangible teaching philosophy begins to emerge. Philip Farkas, who read the rough draft in one sitting, felt that he learned more about the Jacobs theories in that reading than he did during the many years of their association.

The generations of brass players who, in the early years, passed through the Jacobs' living room, dining room, and kitchen on the way to the famous basement, remember with great fondness the hospitality of Mrs. Jacobs. She always made the wait for each lesson seem a little less stressful.

An informal, personal approach seemed to be an appropriate format for an Arnold Jacobs tribute. As I received the responses from each contributor, it was apparent that great care had been taken in the preparation of each memoir. It was therefore decided to do only clean-up editing and then to duplicate the statements in order to preserve the sincerity that was so impressive in the original manuscripts.

The development of the manuscript was due in large part to the great patience and guidance of my family — wife Rozella, son Mark, and daughter Amy. This project has been one of great interest and excitement for me. As Jake reads our efforts, it is my sincere hope that the dedication and devotion of all who contributed is as obvious as the determination they demonstrated in the preparation of the materials.

With profound admiration for the accomplishments of the MASTER, I share with you his real LEGACY — his friends!

M. Dee Stewart

M. Dee Stewart left the Philadelphia Orchestra and the Curtis Institute of Music in 1980 to join the faculty at Indiana University. During his 18 years in Philadelphia, he performed on tenor trombone, bass trombone, tenor tuba, and bass trumpet with the orchestra and made five recordings with the Grammy award-winning Philadelphia Brass Ensemble. He is active as a clinician and recitalist. Mr. Stewart was one of the organizers of the Second International Brass Congress held at Indiana University in 1984.

Arnold Jacobs

I want to thank Dee Stewart in advance for undertaking the thankless job of corralling people who would say a few nice things about me, and for conceiving and carrying out this undertaking. I have deferred all writing and editing to Dee's good judgment. Assuming I get a few complimentary copies, I will call it square on my end — I only hope they don't lose too much money.

I have done my best as a teacher and have tried to be a good friend. My ideas have not always been popular. Right now I am enjoying a rather exalted senior status as a teacher, but I hope my ideas will have some contribution to the pleasure of music-making long after I have finished encouraging my students.

Arnold Jacobs

Ronald Bishop
Tuba, Cleveland Orchestra

Arnold Jacobs is a phenomenon that I'm glad happened to me during my lifetime. He is an example to us all. His influence on me has been profound.

Jacobs' fantastic sound and incredible artistry entered my life through the numerous recordings he has made during his illustrious career. I didn't get to hear him live and actually talk to this living legend until 1958 in Washington, D.C. The Chicago Symphony Orchestra, conducted by Fritz Reiner, was playing Stravinsky, Wagner, and Beethoven in Constitution Hall. I was the typical wide-eyed, awe-struck admirer who just wanted to be near the great man.

My formal work with Mr. Jacobs began in 1959; I'll never forget that first lesson. As I walked up to the old house on South Normal I heard the unmistakable sounds of the master loosening up. That first walk downstairs was a memorable moment. The young lady in the movie *Frankenstein* could not have felt much differently: I saw all those machines, tubes, tubas, mirrors — even a skeleton!

I have the notes from the first lesson, and I'm still trying to put it all together so I can do it as easily as he does, in spite of his physical problems. Jake's range, his range of dynamics, his sound, and his virtuosity have served as my inspiration to this day. To know that he has been doing it all these years with a fuel supply handicap is even more mind boggling.

All of his conductors have recognized his enormous talent. One conductor we both worked for was Josef Krips who was my boss in Buffalo and Jake's guest conductor in Chicago. I recall Krips talking to me after his Chicago Symphony Orchestra engagement. In his thick Viennese accent he said, "Mein Gott, vat a marvelous player is dis Mr. Jacobs. He plays the tuba like it was a violin!" (Krips had conducted a piece by Walton and Jake had dazzled him with his prodigious virtuosity).

Over a 25-year span, relationships change. First Jake was my idol, then my teacher, then my colleague. Now he's my idol, my teacher, my colleague and as always, a role model. The Kamakazi Runs from Buffalo to Chicago through rain, sleet, snow, and ice

1

were always rewarding. I'd return invigorated and renewed.

On my 1963 drive west to assume my post with the San Francisco Symphony, I stopped in Chicago for a lesson. Mr. Jacobs told me that Krips had offered him the job in San Francisco, but he had decided to stay in Chicago. At the end of the lesson, which as usual ran about two hours, Jake jokingly said, "Let's switch — you stay here and I'll go to the coast!" These words came up again in variation around 1966 while I was showing Jake the San Francisco sights. We were standing in the rhododendron dell in Golden Gate Park and he said, "Why do you want to go back east to Cleveland and the snow when you've got a beautiful town and great weather here. Do you think we might exchange jobs?" Jake knew exactly why I wanted to go to the Cleveland Orchestra and Szell: excellence.

Mr. Jacob's career is an example of excellence: the attainment of the best that's in you. It is this quality that is still an inspiration to us all.

The mechanics or technique of playing a wind instrument a la Jacobs could and should fill a book, but that's for Mr. Jacobs to do.

I had a lesson less than two years ago, and I'd have one tomorrow if he'd take me because I want to hear him tell me yet again how easy it is. Furthermore, I need to hear it again so I can pass it on to my students in hopes that they may tell their story the way Arnold Jacobs has been telling his story all these wonderful years.

Stephen Chenette
Instructor of Trumpet, Toronto University

Arnold Jacobs is the most influential brass teacher in the world. This statement is true at the present time, and it is probably true in relation to previous eras. It is difficult to evaluate the influence of brass teachers prior to the 20th century because little has been written about them; but it is unlikely that anyone has had as much influence on brass pedagogy as Arnold Jacobs. Players come to study with him from all over the world, and many of them are already established professionals.

Through research and study, Arnold Jacobs has achieved an understanding of the physiology and psychology of wind instrument playing and is responsible for some fundamental changes in the way brass instruments are played and taught today. He has convincingly demonstrated that the primary mental focus of the performer should be on the musical rather than physical aspects of performing.

The use of air is fundamental to brass playing, and a comparison between Jacobs' teaching and that which I received as a youngster will illustrate the nature of his contributions. A consensus of the instruction that I had from a number of well-meaning teachers and clinicians follows: expand the stomach when taking a breath, but don't raise the chest because the blowing muscles are down low. Before starting a note, make the stomach muscles very firm, and continue to push them out, or down, while playing. Take in only as much air as is needed to play the passage. (The teachers that I had at the Curtis Institute of Music and afterwards are not those responsible for the advice that I am discussing here.)

According to Arnold Jacobs, there is no reason not to take a full breath, which includes a natural expansion of the chest, because the respiratory muscles control all parts of the thoracic cavity (which contains the lungs). Taking as full a breath as is comfortable is recommended by Jacobs, because blowing is easiest when the lungs are full. The elasticity of the lungs, the pull of gravity on an elevated chest, and the torque of the ribs at their points of insertion supplement the action of the expiratory muscles. The less air there is in the lungs, the greater is the degree of effort required by the expiratory muscles to maintain a steady flow of air; this can have a negative effect on the tone and ease of playing.

Firming the abdominal muscles before starting a tone is both unnecessary and unwise, according to Jacobs. He has demonstrated that any degree of air flow can be started at the instant that it is needed, without any prior buildup. If the internal air is compressed before it is time for the note to begin, it must be prevented from reaching the embouchure by either blocking it with the tongue (which can cause a rough attack) or by closing the throat (closed throats can be recalcitrant about opening fully when it is time to play.) If the respiratory muscles are contracted without compressing the internal air, it shows that the inspiratory and expiratory muscles are in isometric contraction, pushing against each other rather than against the lungs. When it is time for the note to start, the inspiratory muscles will, to a sometimes considerable degree, continue to resist as the expiratory muscles try to decrease the size of the thoracic cavity. The problems this can cause show up most vividly in high and loud playing.

Air is exhaled only as the thoracic cavity decreases in size, and the only meaningful activity of the respiratory muscles is that which causes this to happen. Consciously trying to push out or down with the abdominal muscles while playing works against the physical necessities of the body, and causes a conflict between the conscious and subconscious mind (which knows exactly what must be done).

Jacobs' research has included studies of the variations of internal air pressure of wind players, and he has noted a significant difference between woodwind and brass players. Both must vary air pressure to change volume, but brass players must also do it to change registers, with air pressure more or less doubling to ascend one octave. The idea of maintaining constant abdominal muscular tension conflicts with the necessity of constantly varying air pressures while playing a brass instrument.

While his knowledge of the physical aspects of brass playing is unsurpassed and his contributions in this area are invaluable, even more helpful are Arnold Jacobs' teachings on the mental aspects of playing. He stresses that while it is desirable to understand the physical basis of playing, it is impossible to control the use of the air (or other parts of playing) adequately by conscious thought. There is simply not enough sensory information available to the conscious brain to make this possible, and the mechanics of respiration, like so many other aspects of wind playing, are best left to the subconscious. The performer should picture in his mind what should happen and leave it to the subconscious to take care of the details. This idea does not sound at all revolutionary in the 1980s, but Arnold Jacobs has been teaching this way for over 40 years.

I first met Arnold Jacobs in the fall of 1952, when I was 16 years old. At the mid-point of a train trip from my home in a small New Mexico town to Philadelphia, where I was to begin studying at the Curtis Institute of Music, I stopped in Chicago for a few days to see the sights of a big city. I went to museums, my first major league baseball games, and the Sonja Henie Ice Show. I was eager to meet some real professional musicians, and I headed for the bandstand at the ice show at the first break. The man with the tuba was the easiest to spot. I wish that I could recall more of what we talked about, but I do remember that Mr. Jacobs was kind and charming to a very naive teenager. One of the regrets of my life is that 10 years passed before I had my first lesson from him.

I grew up thinking that some people were naturals who could play a brass instrument efficiently and easily, while the rest of us had to work hard at it. When I joined the Minnesota Orchestra (then called the Minneapolis Symphony), there were some players in the brass section who seemed to qualify as naturals, but I came to realize that they had all studied with Arnold Jacobs. So, towards the end of my second season with the orchestra, with some important recording sessions imminent, I called and scheduled a couple of lessons. In those days, before the brass players of the world were beating a path to his door, it was much simpler to arrange lessons.

Mr. Jacobs was still teaching at his home at 8839 South Normal, and anyone who went to that house will never forget it. It was unpretentious, and the best words to describe the interior are warm and full. It was full of furniture, magazines, sewing projects, tropical fish, and Schweppes. Schweppes could have made an empty house seem full. He was a small, aggressive dog who saw it as his duty to inform the world that I was an obviously shady character who had no business being anywhere in the vicinity, especially not inside the house. A doorbell at 8839 South Normal was completely unnecessary, because my first footstep on the front porch aroused in Schweppes a surge of vigilance that often continued until I was out of his domain and into the music room.

5

The music room was in the basement at the front of the house, and was reached by going down stairs at the back and through a narrow pathway in a combination laundry and storeroom. Reaching the music room was like entering another world. It was full too, but full of musical and scientific equipment and books. I couldn't begin to list everything, but the collection was awesome. (It seems to me that a relatively small percentage of the collection was installed in the new studio when Mr. Jacobs began teaching downtown.) For me, this room became the Mecca where the truths of brass playing were to be revealed.

If a mind can be boggled, mine certainly was in those first lessons. The basic ideas that I had been taught about muscle manipulation in general, and breathing and breath support in particular, were shown to be incorrect, but shown in such a clear, logical, and scientific way that one could not fail to be utterly convinced. Jacobs' basic message was so simple and natural that I wondered why I'd never thought of it myself. (I, and many thousands of others, never had.) There was an immediate improvement in my playing, and I received compliments from colleagues in the Minnesota Orchestra who knew nothing about the lessons. Simply taking full rather than partial breaths, and not consciously tightening the abdominal muscles made my playing considerably easier.

In the early lessons, Mr. Jacobs tested me on various items of equipment: vital capacity, flow rate of air during exhalation, and static breath pressure measurements are the main ones that I remember. I didn't play much that first day; in fact, I rarely played much in a lesson. A few lines of a study or solo were enough for him to analyze my problems and needs. He was extremely informative, always explaining the rationale of things that he asked me to do, and his command of language, especially in technical matters, was incredible. I have to smile when I recall how he would speak for a while in flawlessly constructed paragraphs (which could have been incorporated verbatim into the book that his students hope he will write) and then look at me and say, "You dig?"

Mr. Jacobs used equipment not only for measurement, but also for practice routines to institute new or improved ways of playing. His drills were not mechanical because he always made the students see the underlying musical purpose. Blowing or playing into some sort of gauge has the advantage of focusing attention on an external object, rather than internal physical processes, and also gives an immediate evaluation of how successful one is.

The quantity and quality of Jacobs' knowledge is only the first part of his mastery as a teacher. He can, of course, explain himself with amazing clarity, but the greatest aspect of his teaching is the way he can show students how to retrain their own playing. He has an incredible variety of practice routines, both with and without an instrument, and a sure knowledge of what to use when.

The first phase of my study with Arnold Jacobs, which lasted several years, was learning his approach to brass playing. Later, there was a period when I would see him for checkups, although he usually taught me new things, too. Most recently, after several years of full-time teaching and minimal performing, I found that I was thinking as a teacher even during my own playing, and falling victim to what Jacobs calls "paralysis by analysis." The third, and current, phase of my study with Arnold Jacobs is concerned with focusing my mind away from the internal physical responses and onto the external musical result. This was nothing new because Jacobs had this as a primary goal right from my first lesson with him, but now the physical information he imparted has receded far into the background. The challenge now is to discover and use those thought processes and mental images which will cause the subconscious parts of the brain to make the desired physical activities happen. Jacobs stresses that detailed physical knowledge is relatively unimportant to the act of performing.

Arnold Jacobs knows how the body works while playing a wind instrument, but, more important, he knows what the mind must do to get the body to work well. From complex knowledge he has distilled a simplicity of approach which offers all of us the possibility of becoming natural players. The essence of this simplicity is to conceive of brass playing in terms of song and wind.

Daniel P. Corrigan
Tuba, Indianapolis Symphony

My first contact with Arnold Jacobs took place in 1951 when I was a freshman at DePaul University in Chicago. I had just started playing in Renold Schilke's brass ensemble, and he suggested Mr. Jacobs to me as a private instructor. It was the beginning of a relationship that was to shape my entire musical life.

Getting to Arnold Jacobs' house proved to be a problem in itself. He lived on the far southside, 8800 south, and I lived on the northside, 3200 north. I had no car and was forced to rely on public transportation. This entailed taking an elevated train, transferring to a streetcar, and then transferring to a bus. After departing the bus there was still a two-block walk to his home. All this was done carrying a tuba. The trip was approximately one hour and 45 minutes each way. Add to this the lesson time and it is easy to see why my lessons with Mr. Jacobs were an important part of each week.

Back in the 1950s Arnold Jacobs was not as well known as a teacher and did not have as many students. This gave him more time for each student. My first few lessons exceeded two hours each.

Living in Chicago gave me many opportunities to observe and associate with Arnold Jacobs and his other students. I heard the Chicago Symphony every chance I could. Being at a university that was in close proximity to such a great orchestra provided educational opportunities seldom found anywhere. Several of us made the weekly pilgrimage from 64 East Lake to Orchestra Hall. We had a class that ended at 2:00 p.m., and then we would run six blocks at full speed, purchase our tickets, and rush up the five flights of stairs to arrive in time for the first note. Hearing Arnold Jacobs in those concerts gave me a concept of beautiful sound that I still consider the ideal.

My association with many of his students was also very close because they literally lived with my family. We own a two-flat building in Chicago and rented rooms in the flat on the second floor. Finding a place to practice, especially for a low brass player, pre-

8

sents problems, and we were happy to be able to resolve some of them. We had as many as four students living upstairs at one time. Several symphonies and university faculties had representatives who stayed at our home while studying with Arnold Jacobs. Some of the names that come to mind are Steve Zellmer (Minneapolis Symphony), Paul Walton (formerly Minneapolis Symphony), Gene Isaif (formerly Minneapolis Symphony), Ardash Marderosian (Lyric Opera and Grant Park Symphony), and many others. At almost any time of the day or evening you could hear someone practicing, and during informal get-togethers, we would discuss aspects of Jacobs' teaching. The opportunity to practice at will and hear others striving for the same goals was greatly appreciated by all who stayed at our house, myself included. However, I must admit this was not always as appreciated by some of the residents of the apartment building next door.

When I reflect on Mr. Jacobs' teaching over the years the first concept that comes to mind is breathing — the concept that healthy breathing will produce a healthy embouchure. The reverse is equally true — when the mass and flow of air are insufficient, problems will appear such as those with embouchure, tonguing, and so on. One very simple rule of Mr. Jacobs' is that in order to release a sufficient quantity of air you must take in a large enough quantity of air. This means that the entire chest and diaphragm must be relaxed and able to expand and contract freely with each breath.

We also discussed the many ways our bodies can fool us by sending back signals of work when the results do not match the effort. The negative respiratory curve is a perfect example. You think you are still blowing the same amount of air, but when measured, the amount actually being released is far less than you think. His thorough knowledge of physiology gave him great insight into breathing problems, and his detailed explanations would be material for a scholarly thesis.

While Mr. Jacobs is probably most famous for his concept of breathing, I feel his most important contribution to my development was the concept of "mentalizing" — the idea that you must have a mental image of the end result before you can achieve it. There must be a brass instrument in your mind playing the way you want to sound. Any playing you do should be an attempt to make the sound that comes out of your bell match what you are conceiving in your mind. We can't go by listen and feel. We can't

9

play a note blindly and then make judgments as to whether we liked it or not. Once a sound has been played it is too late. True control exists in the mental picture before the sound is produced. When the mental picture is correct and the proper concentration is present, the body will perform all the necessary functions to get the job done. Good brass playing is a matter of training the mind to conceptualize and concentrate. It sounds easy but we all know it isn't.

My study with Arnold Jacobs continues to the present day. Although we have not had formal lessons for a few years, I talk to him often when I am in Chicago. I still seek his advice — advice that I treasure and try to share with all my students.

Arnold Jacobs teaching   Rich Mays

10

Eugene Dowling
Tuba, Victoria Symphony

A common thread runs through numerous conversations that I've had with musicians who have studied with Arnold Jacobs. Many of them repeat the phrase "I wouldn't be playing now if it weren't for Mr. Jacobs." He has made careers possible for many musicians as well as prolonged the careers of countless others. His own record of over 50 years as an orchestral tubist speaks to the success of his approach.

In the summer of 1969 I first went to Arnold Jacobs to study because of the tremendous reputation he enjoyed as a pedagogue, particularly in the areas of breathing and tone production. I was at Michigan State University at the time, and my teacher, Leonard Falcone, encouraged me to go to Chicago. I had first heard the Reiner/Chicago recording of the Bartok *Concerto for Orchestra* in high school. When that tone of immense weight and depth emerged from the speakers during the chorale sections, I knew immediately that that was how a tuba should sound. It is difficult to describe nearly 20 years later, but listening to that sound erased years of ignorance and perhaps frightened me by how much there was left to understand.

In my first lesson I must have played all of 12 notes while we worked on breathing. As anyone who has experienced the environment of his studio knows, the first lesson is one of sensory overstimulation. It is simply impossible to comprehend the depth of his knowledge that first time. Your mind simply becomes an open vessel to receive the larger points he is making. He insists on relaxed, open playing combined with the highest musical standards. A student often wanders out of a lesson after listening to more information than he can possibly absorb. Often, he can only remember a key phrase like "wind and song." I believe that this is Jacobs' intent because these phrases serve as a summing up of his approach and distill the essence of his message. I studied with him sporadically until I went to work with him in Chicago and studied with him at Northwestern University and later through the Civic Orchestra of Chicago. My playing improved a great deal during this time and laid the groundwork for my professional life.

11

Much of my later work with Mr. Jacobs involved achieving a consistent approach to playing during practice and in performance. Someone once told me that Mr. Jacobs' teaching was actually as valuable, if not more so, in later life when we experience the actual demands of a job. The numerous professionals securely holding jobs is a testimony to that statement.

Something Mr. Jacobs' pulled on a number of the students working with him during the time I was in Chicago was to say, " You should have heard X's lesson last week" and "Y is sounding like a god these days. I've never heard you sound better, either." Turning to you with a sly grin and hitting you on the shoulder he'd say, "Of course, I still play better than any of you!"

Of course, he's absolutely right.

Arnold Jacobs, taken by Philip Farkas, c. 1959

Richard H. Erb
Bass Trombone, New Orleans Symphony

I met Arnold Jacobs in the spring of 1966. Probably many players, in describing their own first meetings with him, refer to those events as having had "a profound effect." I believe that no one can make that statement with more certain conviction than I. All that has been rewarding as a performer and teacher in my career since that time has been possible because of this remarkable man.

At the time I met Mr. Jacobs, I was 29 years old and had been a professional player for about five years. I had just completed my second year in the New Orleans Philharmonic. Prior to that I had played for two years in the San Antonio Symphony. The year before that I was completing my studies at Carnegie-Mellon University in Pittsburgh, and had been fortunate to have a fair amount of extra work with the Pittsburgh Symphony, as well as other engagements in that area.

My training before 1966 was entirely in the Pittsburgh area, largely with players associated with the Symphony. Those who influenced me most were Byron McCulloh and Carl Wilhelm. Both are outstanding players, and in addition to providing inspiration and an excellent artistic model, they were extremely dedicated and supportive teachers. Beyond that, both became close personal friends, and provided me role-models on both a human and professional level. I remain deeply grateful for their patience and encouragement. Without them I could not have hoped to enter the profession at all.

What was it that led me to seek further help, and from a source with quite different background and methods, at a relatively advanced point in my own development? Many professional players continue to seek and strive for something a little better in their work, and I hope that I was among that group at that time, but quite honestly I was also goaded a bit by the curious realization that the work was not getting any easier in spite of a modestly growing store of experience. There seemed to be a tiny worm somewhere in the core of my sound production.

Getting the particular job (New Orleans) at the time I did (1964) can only be described as a fantastic piece of luck. There I found the most congenial and excellent colleagues one could hope for. The other trombonists were Glenn Dodson and Gordon Sweeney. The tubist was Ross Tolbert, a student of Mr. Jacobs, and an outstanding player. He was, as were the others, an extremely sensitive and supportive person to work with, and when I began to have some misgivings about what I was doing, he was both considerate and generous in sharing some of the insights he had gained in his study with Mr. Jacobs.

One of the things that struck me early in my discussions with Ross concerned Mr. Jacobs' ability to quickly analyze a player's work, particularly the physical aspects of playing. I felt (and continue to feel) that the musical aspects of my prior training and experience had been quite good, but the physical act of producing sound was somewhat mysterious to me, and was becoming more rather than less so.

When I did begin to study with Mr. Jacobs at the end of my second year in the orchestra in New Orleans, I was astonished to find that not only had Ross's claims been justified, they were far too modest. What seems most striking about the experience is that my study with Mr. Jacobs caused me to reassess the entire question of what musical ability, talent if you will, really consists of, and how teaching relates to it.

Playing a brass instrument well requires the mastery of at least two large areas or disciplines. In a very general view they could be described in this way. One consists of all the physical and sensory phenomena which cooperate in producing organized, controlled sound. The other is the artistic, expressive aspect of music-making, which is best described as a conceptual skill. One must, at least in symphonic playing (or interpreting), take a set of cues relevant to the sense of sight — the printed page — and convert them into a set of cues relevant to and experienced by the sense of hearing. To do this requires something nearly magical: the ability to conceptualize sound before it exists physically. It is rare that a player's mastery in these two widely differing areas is exactly balanced. It is also important to remember that as a student develops, these two aspects rarely develop at the same rate, and any assessment of potential must take into account this relationship.

14

One unique quality in Mr. Jacobs' teaching, however, is his degree of understanding of the two-sided, physical/conceptual nature of performing. This awareness is what has enabled him, in my opinion, to make his teaching so effective. It also encourages an acute awareness of the question of motivation. It is clear that in successful playing each of the two aspects participates, the physical/sensory or mechanical aspect, and the conceptual/artistic aspect. Mr. Jacobs has used this device of recognizing the separateness of these aspects to allow him to apply his vast knowledge of learning or behavioral psychology in a way that I believe is unique. He defines the imagined musical idea as the cue that will and must elicit the correct response from the physical side of the player.

Before going further, let me say that Mr. Jacobs himself might object to some of the above. He might protest that his way of teaching concentrates almost entirely on the idea of "the product (music) as motivation." It is true that whenever possible he stresses that while playing one must concentrate on the desired (conceptualized) musical statement. The mental processes of the performer must not be occupied by thoughts (particularly verbal thoughts) of method. He might object that my description of what he did in my case tends to stress the physical response side too much, or elevate it to a position of equality with the other, conceptual aspect. Let me say only that I am attempting to describe my perception of my own experience as a student. These are my subjective observations of what I believe he is and was doing, and I have not discussed them with him in this particularly broad way.

When I began my study with Mr. Jacobs, I thought that I was seeking the solution to a single narrowly defined physical problem relating to attacks. I was astonished at his enormous store of information of a purely scientific nature — anatomical, physiological, as well as behavioral. I had a general awareness that most of this information existed, but I never (age 29!) made the connection between it and playing. Some individuals seem to begin playing as youngsters with a minimum of physical effort or awkwardness, while others take three years to get a recognizable sound over a range wider than a fifth; unfortunately, I was in the latter group. Some possible factors may be a general high level of physical athletic ability, excellent coordination, or strong kinesthetic senses. Another factor may be the absence of bad instruction in breathing. As a teacher I have found that pupils who come to me relatively or largely self-taught rarely have truly incorrect breathing habits. Brass players have inherited a legacy of misinformation regarding this. My own guess is that much of it is a distortion of 19th-century singing techniques passed on to us through (probably further distorted) descriptions by the great band virtuosos of the turn of the century.

In any case I believe Mr. Jacobs was the first teacher or researcher to apply general scientific knowledge of the structure and function of the pulmonary system to brass playing. He was the first, as far as I know, to realize that the most natural function of that system is the most effective way to move air, thus producing a vibration in the embouchure and ultimately music. Other teachers seemed to assume that some exotic maneuvers, used only while playing were necessary; movements or techniques that applied only to brass playing. Their techniques were poorly articulated (if at all) and considered mysterious. The problems were addressed but not solved in this way: the teacher would play or sing an example and say, "OK, like that." My ability to imitate, basically a conceptual skill, was pretty good. Success or failure to produce a similar result was, I suppose, considered a measure of talent, and the lack of it couldn't be fixed anyhow. Little information of the sort describing the method ever changed hands. After all, the ability to execute an action does not assure the ability to describe it. Thus, I was amazed when Mr. Jacobs was able to not only demonstrate, but describe each separate component of each complex action involved in playing. Further he was able to describe not only the action but the cue or stimulus that elicited it.

There has been much discussion of why Mr. Jacobs' psychology, or his use of it, is so effective. My belief is that apart from his obviously positive attitude and his generous encouragement of his students, his method is neither complex nor mysterious. I referred above to cues and responses. This terminology comes from the behaviorist school of psychology, of which B. F. Skinner is probably the best-known writer and researcher. Obviously it is a complex subject, but it can be made useful, or applied, with a very modest amount of background. Once the simple learning paradigm (cue/response/reward) is understood as a way of explaining habits (problems?) or of acquiring new patterns of behavior (learning), progress can be rapid.

16

This is particularly important to a person who, as so many have, comes to Mr. Jacobs while already engaged as a professional. That was my situation in 1966; and while the changes he created in my playing were profound, his way of making them was never disruptive. This is another aspect of his teaching that is unique. None of this "take off six months, and then move into my house for a year" stuff!

Although I originally consulted Mr. Jacobs to solve what I thought was a rather minor problem in my sound production, I discovered that the problem was far from minor, and solving it affected every aspect of my playing. My first experience of problem solving with Mr. Jacobs will illustrate some of my observations of his methods.

The problem which so vexed and alarmed me as to send me to an admittedly famous stranger in Chicago was difficulty in starting the initial note in a phrase. It was not as drastic as this sounds, just a tendency to lateness, a reluctance on the part of the tongue to move on rhythmic command. It was only apparent outside of the rhythmic context supplied by an ensemble, and particularly so on the dreaded first note of the day. That was always B♭ of course, since the Remington warmup starts that way, and my devotion to it was religious or obsessive depending on one's viewpoint. Various people suggested various remedies, mostly psychological (in the sense of positive thinking) or artistic. When I described the problem which by then had concerned me for four or five years, Mr. Jacobs described the specific cause and the specific cure in a matter of minutes — before he heard or saw me play a note!

I think it is worth sharing a bit of the technical aspects of this for several reasons. First, no one else had even the vaguest notion what to do about it. Curiously, I have had some discussions with other students of Mr. Jacobs and none relate a similar problem or having any awareness of such a problem. This is surprising because I have observed this phenomenon in the general population of brass players with considerable frequency.

The cause of the difficulty is simply the presence of static air, held under pressure in the lungs by the closing off by tongue, lips, or glottis. When the lungs are full, the diaphragm is, of course, in its downward contracted position. When the top of the system is closed, great pressure in the lungs may be generated by the opposing (to the diaphragm) musculature of the abdominal wall. This also results in greatly increased pressure on the contents of the abdominal cavity. When this pressure is sensed and processed in the brain, the autonomic nervous system reacts in a typical pattern of behavior known to physiologists as the Valsalva Maneuver. (Valsalva (1666-1723) was the Italian anatomist and physiologist who first described this phenomenon.) Simply put, the response has this effect: the diaphragm maintains or increases the downward pressure or contraction. The tongue maintains a simultaneous effort to block the airway, thus maintaining internal pressure. Now while the diaphragm's primary function is one of inhalation, this secondary or supportive use of it is essential to the body in several functions such as emptying the bowel or bladder or in childbirth. The crucial point to understand is that this pattern of responses is triggered through the autonomic nervous system and therefore totally beyond one's conscious control. The tongue at that moment of high internal pressure will not respond to a conscious command to begin a note.

Many players never encounter this difficulty, but certain factors commonly encountered in traditional brass pedagogy and method books may create a situation where it will occur. For example, any variation of the instruction, "Build up your air pressure behind the tongue in order to prepare for the attack," may cause the beginning of the difficulty. In any case, such an instruction, which is fairly commonly encountered, is an inaccurate description of the situation that should prevail in the instant before the attack. Another problem is the tendency of many teachers (some of the fine players who should know better) to instruct students not to raise the upper chest in inhaling, but to use something utterly erroneously referred to as the diaphragm. When used in this erroneous way, this term is usually taken to mean a general area, roughly around the waistline, rather than a single muscle. This matter is often discussed in conjunction with something generally referred to as support. This term is also without scientific or other definition, but it seems in practice to have several connotations that result in isometric tension or rigidity in the abdominal wall.

The three concepts of pedagogy mentioned above (air pressure for preparation, diaphragmatic breathing, and support) taken together almost perfectly describe the condition in which the Valsalva Maneuver will be triggered. Individuals vary in their sensitivity to this as they do in other reflexes. In my case I have a high degree of sensitivity to this response.

Mr. Jacobs' method of dealing with the problem was direct and straightforward. I had three one-hour sessions over a period of two weeks. After observing my playing, he gave me a general but concise overview of the anatomy of the thorax and abdomen, referring to the large charts and models in his studio. Armed with this information (almost all of it new to me) he explained in detail the physiological phenomenon known as the Valsalva Maneuver. The vast amount of new material in that first half of the first session was not presented in any simplified or watered-down version. After having explained and demonstrated the correct way of dealing with beginning a note, he worked on these new concepts with the aid of several mechanical devices. Mr. Jacobs uses these devices for two reasons: first they allow an utterly objective analysis of air movement, body movement, and the relationship of the two. Second, they provide striking new cues — cues not carrying any anxiety-producing emotional or judgmental baggage — to elicit new responses. This can result in far faster learning than any traditional, purely musical, method. Mr. Jacobs was quick to point out that we were looking for ways to alter behavior as quickly and non-disruptively as possible. At the time, I was only able to spend about two weeks in Chicago because of my work. He told me that if I were there long-term, he would rely far less on these aids and would approach all problems from the standpoint of using pure musical ideas as the stimulus. He recognized, however, that my situation was not ideal, and we proceeded from the ideal to the practical.

The devices used were the spirometer, pneumograph bands, several gauges to measure air flow and air pressure, and the oscilloscope. The spirometer was of the air-storing variety, measuring how much air I could move, and with a tank for storing specific measured quantities of air for later use. The three pneumograph bands were placed as follows: high around chest (just under the armpits), bottom edge of the rib cage (10th rib), and approximately at the waist (across the navel). Each band was connected to a small gauge that showed any expansion or contraction in body size. A correct breath would therefore cause motion in all three areas, but the motion would be in the same general direction and synchronized in time. It was possible to see instantly the pattern of motion connected to each breath. In my prior training the visible motion of the body during breathing was rarely discussed, except that large movements in the upper rib cage were discouraged. Much of the work with Mr. Jacobs was done playing on the mouthpiece only, another new idea to me. Apart from the obvious benefits of this type of practice, it had the effect of removing the most potent cue likely to trigger old habits — the trombone itself. I believe that while teaching Mr. Jacobs analyzes every stimulus acting upon the student from the standpoint of cue/response/reward. He is consciously and methodically altering behavior at all times.

He stressed that using the pneumograph, which measures only body movement, is valid only in conjunction with some means of measuring air flow. Sound coming from an instrument is one way, but we wanted some way to measure flow (result) without cues that would elicit old responses. Therefore he used a simple set-up of rubber tubes, some with ports, which led to flow meters we could observe. The combination of visual read-out of body movement and visual read-out of air flow rates, free of old cues (trombone), allowed near ideal breathing performance to be experienced very quickly.

The next step was to try to transfer these new responses to the trombone. Still pursuing the original problem of delayed, paralyzed attacks, Mr. Jacobs used a device to measure air pressure inside the oral cavity during playing and also before the note began. He also used a mouthpiece with a port for a tube to a pressure gauge to measure pressure in the cup simultaneously.

We discovered that in the last moments of silence before the sound began I was generating enormous pressures in the oral cavity, caused by the accidental triggering of the Valsalva Maneuver. Without the understanding of this physiology, it would have been absolutely impossible to solve this problem. With this information the problem can be solved without the mechanical equipment, but far less quickly. The action of read-out equipment serves as a strong, clearly recognizable reward for new behavior. Mr. Jacobs clearly understands the fact that a negative reward induces the very behavior one is trying to extinguish. How few teachers understand this. He also said that "the subconscious does not understand 'not' " — his way of recognizing the futility of admonishing a student not to do something. This is clearly in conformity with behaviorist theory.

Let me stress, however, that no awareness of psychological theory on the part of the student is necessary. My limited knowledge of it is useful to me in writing or in explaining his methods, but was of no real use in altering my responses during those first three lessons. The method does not depend on the education or the intellectual capacity of the student. In fact, Mr. Jacobs suggested that my own rather analytical nature was probably a disadvantage in my playing.

As I reflect now on this experience I am struck by the directness of his approach. As I pursued study with him over the next 17 years, there were times when he made changes without much conscious awareness of them on my part, but at the beginning he was specific and direct. He was sensitive to the fact that I had a job and had to continue playing on an acceptable professional level while he altered things in my sound production. Nothing he did was disruptive, nor did it involve any need to interrupt my normal activity in playing. Rather its effect was to add to what I could do almost from the first lesson. The most profound effect, which 17 years later is still as clear and pronounced as it was then, was a feeling of enormous relief: relief from anxiety, relief from what seemed like the domination of irrational, inexplicable forces. If that seems overly dramatic as a statement, remember that my body was doing something I didn't want it to do, and I didn't know why. When I discovered that not only this phenomenon, but any other that a player is likely to encounter, could be explained in scientific and quantifiable ways by a person of the highest artistic and scientific integrity, then the prospect of learning to play became far less frightening. Once and for all it had been demystified. I cannot stress enough that before I knew of this enormous body of knowledge, I (and my teachers) could only explain success or failure in terms of industry, application, and that utterly unquantifiable term "Talent." Used in this context talent meant something like predestination. If everything worked perfectly, you had it. If it didn't, well then you didn't, and you'd have to make do the best you could in an element to which you were obviously ill suited.

Time and space (and readers' patience) will prevent me from dealing with later lessons in the same detail as the first three. My way of studying with Mr. Jacobs has of necessity been in short periods on a roughly annual basis because I never had the opportunity to live in Chicago for any extended period of time.

In June 1967 I returned to Chicago. During the year since my first sessions I had made tremendous progress. My entire way of breathing had changed, and the problem of delayed or unmanageable attacks was gone. My whole attitude towards my work was different, and far more positive. Many problems remained to be dealt with, but I felt that none of them had to be tolerated because the means were at my disposal to deal with them.

Mr. Jacobs apparently felt I had done well at solving the problems we had dealt with in my first sessions, and I was comfortable with him and with his way of working. I suppose as a result of this, and of his personal kindness and understanding, an opportunity presented itself to me that has led to the most rewarding association of my professional life.

In 1968 Mr. Jacobs agreed to teach the lower brass for the National Youth Orchestra of Canada. This is, and was then, one of the finest organizations of its type in the world; and they assembled an outstanding international faculty. Unfortunately, Mr. Jacobs became ill in late June, only a short time before their session was to begin. The administration of the N.Y.O. was accustomed to engaging persons whose names were household words in our profession, but when confronted with the problem of finding a replacement for Mr. Jacobs, they were understandably at a loss. They discussed the problem with him, and he suggested three of his students for their consideration, persons he felt had some understanding of his methods and a suitable personality for teaching advanced students.

Two of those suggested were playing at the highest level of the profession in prestigious orchestras. The third, to my lasting amazement, was me. Obviously the others, contacted first, were unavailable, but my availability in summer on short notice was high. The call from the National Youth Orchestra of Canada to me was probably one of the strangest of its kind in history. They had no idea who I was, but their regard for Mr. Jacobs' recommendation was so high that they took a chance and hired me. I knew less about them than they knew about me. All I could tell them was that the crabs in Lake Pontchartrain would be as grateful as I was for anything that would occupy my attention elsewhere.

I still work there. A lot has happened in those rewarding summers. None of it would have involved me without Mr. Jacobs' kind recommendation, but there are, I think, larger considerations. First, I tried from the beginning to base my own teaching there on his methods, particularly his psychological approach. Second and more important, many of the brass students there found themselves influenced by and attracted to the style of playing and teaching available in Chicago from Mr. Jacobs and other members of the orchestra there. Today, a large number of the finest young Canadian players have gone to Chicago for their studies. In recent years, it is always the case that several members of the brass section of the N.Y.O./Canada are either current or former students of Mr. Jacobs or his colleagues in the Chicago Symphony.

A few years ago we were fortunate to add Vincent Cichowicz to our faculty. Mr. Cichowicz, of course, was a colleague of Mr. Jacobs for many years in the Chicago Symphony, and he has added enormously to our program. I believe that his outstanding teaching methods also were influenced by Mr. Jacobs, so that Jacobs' influence has pervaded that program even though we have never been fortunate enough to have him there personally. I am proud of the work I have done there, but my students and I have never lost sight of the fact that Mr. Jacobs has remained the guiding force in what we have accomplished. In every sense he made it all possible for me, and for them as well.

I will now try to deal briefly with some of the further pedagogical details of what I have worked on in the years since 1968. After solving the enigma of the Valsalva Maneuver, and establishing full-capacity breathing, free from isometric tension, I next faced the problem of the tongue itself being in the wrong place, both in articulation and during the duration of the note. Until my second set of lessons (1967) I always started notes with my tongue through my teeth, and often through my lips as well. One might well ask, "What must that have sounded like?" I suppose that the answer could be "not as bad as it should have." Here again, the musical stimulus of what I wanted my attacks to sound like was clear and strong enough that I could get by with it. The problems were more often manifested in terms of reliability than in what it sounded like when it worked. It also served to exacerbate the problems related to delayed attacks caused by triggering the Valsalva Maneuver.

Incorrect tongue placement after the attack was related to the problems described above. My tongue remained not in the formation similar to an "O" vowel, but farther forward in the mouth, almost in a position similar to the sibilant consonant "S." These two related difficulties were attacked in a way that again demonstrates Mr. Jacobs' psychological approach. These drastic changes were made away from the instrument because having the trombone in one's hand is a powerful, emotionally charged cue. It will elicit whatever response has been rewarded in the past. Mr. Jacobs always stressed that whatever is learned is learned forever. One cannot unlearn anything, nor can one break a habit. Once cue/ response/reward takes place, nothing can eliminate or erase the effect, short of a time machine. This does not mean that change is impossible. New learning can occur at any time, just as earlier behavior was learned.

To facilitate this, an entirely new set of cues and carefully selected responses, systematically rewarded, is needed. Applied to the problem described, it worked like this: new learning was started away from the instrument with mouthpiece or practice ring only. Mr. Jacobs pointed out the unconscious ease with which we speak. Vocal sounds are produced under perfect control, without any conscious effort or control. The responses which form speech-sounds are motivated by the sounds (words) being conceptualized in the brain in a way that exactly parallels ideal playing. He therefore constructed speech patterns I had mastered by age two, which paralleled the movements required to begin a note properly. Using these new cues, he then began to transfer the new way of starting notes to the instrument, but now always using speech patterns to motivate correct movements. In a similar way he then changed the shape of my oral cavity while playing, through the relation to and imitation of vowel sounds. At this time he explained the relationship of the Bernoulli Principle to tongue position.

While this is essential information for proper and efficient sound production, particularly in the high register, we never based work purely on the exchange of information. Rather, the method was more related to behavior modification through his conscious application of behavioral psychology. It is interesting to consider that I had known my tongue was in the wrong position in attacks for many years. I pointed out this fault to my early teachers and wanted to change it, but I could not, with help or alone, in spite of endless worry and some considerable effort. Mr. Jacobs enabled me to change this in a matter of a few weeks.

In trying to bring back these experiences, I have gradually become aware of one unique aspect of Mr. Jacobs' teaching. Apart from his enormous knowledge, which no student of his has ever fully acquired, he has specific pedagogic skills that are what make his teaching so effective. In other words, it is clearly desirable to acquire information, but the acquisition of it is not what causes the dramatic improvements his students experience. It is, in fact, possible to make large changes under Mr. Jacobs' guidance without any intellectual understanding of his factual data whatsoever. He cautions against analyzing one's playing too closely. He has also occasionally suggested that too much time spent analyzing my own students' problems might be less than constructive for my playing.

In visits during subsequent years, we dealt with problems relating to constriction in the throat, in the pharyngeal area. Over a period of time he also made substantial changes in my embouchure, but this was done with such subtlety, starting from the time of my first lessons, that I cannot report when it actually occurred. Embouchure change as such was never discussed, nor was any disruption involved. Not only is the placement different now, quite nearly 50/50 upper/lower, as opposed to perhaps 70/30 upper/lower, but pressure is nearly equal on all 360° of rim surface. The movement in placement was never directly discussed. These changes have greatly relieved another serious problem, that of substantial shifts in position between middle and high register embouchure settings. These shifts, apart from being fairly gross maneuvers, were taking place at far too low a pitch level, long before high register settings were necessary or appropriate.

There are clearly at least two topics or areas which are lacking in this discussion and Mr. Jacobs might object strenuously to their absence. I have, at embarrassing length, discussed my own physical ineptitude and my inability to deal with it unaided. I have tried to explain what I perceive to be Mr. Jacobs' way of causing learning in his students, or at least some of his students. I have said practically nothing about purely musical, or interpretive, or stylistic training.

The truth is, my needs were so great, and the time to deal with them so short during any given period of study, that Mr. Jacobs was forced to use methods he described as short cuts. While only my early sessions involved scientific instruments, the overwhelming majority of time was spent on production rather than on artistic or interpretive matters. Mr. Jacobs told me on several occasions that he was not entirely happy with this, and that had I been able to live in Chicago for an extended period, he would have approached my case differently, in a manner involving far more musical motivation.

While it should by now be apparent that I am deeply grateful for the help and experience that I had, I feel that my general level of artistry would be much higher with that opportunity. Even as things worked out, I received enormous musical inspiration from

25

Mr. Jacobs. This came not only through our association in the lesson, but by hearing him play in the Chicago Symphony at every opportunity. Sadly, inspiration and instruction are not quite the same. There is a sheer musical energy which is reflected in and radiates from his very personality, which affects every one of us who have studied with him. No one can truly copy his unique style. One may be profoundly influenced or guided by him, but all attempts to duplicate fall to the level of caricature.

In this article I have not shed much light on the human side of the man. He always treats me with kindness and warmth, and has the ability to make each student feel special and cared for. His kindness in recommending me to the National Youth Orchestra of Canada altered my career, and I cannot imagine a sufficient expression of gratitude. I have tried to do my work there in a way that would be satisfactory to him, given my own limitations. The only personal advice I can remember receiving was a caution not to try to emulate every detail of his professional life, not to work too hard, to enjoy my family, to remember that sitting under a tree is good for your playing too. I wish I had listened better to him.

Arnold Jacobs, taken by Jerry Sirucek

Philip Farkas
French Horn, Indiana University

How well I remember my first acquaintance with Arnold Jacobs. Before this meeting I had joined the Chicago Symphony in 1936 and, after five years, had gone to the Cleveland Orchestra and then to the Boston Symphony. Upon returning to the Chicago Symphony in 1947, there was a new tubist, Arnold Jacobs. It was my privilege, as the first hornist, to sit almost directly in front of him. Never had I heard such playing, and I sat in front of some very good tuba players. Here was an artist who had subtlety, intonation, dynamic range, tone, rhythm, and above all, phrasing and superb musicianship. To hear Jake breathe (and you had to listen very carefully, even from my close proximity) was a lesson in the physics and mechanics of breathing as well as a lesson in the art of phrasing. I can certainly claim, just by having been in such a wonderful position to observe his artistry, that I am truly a student of Arnold Jacobs.

Jake always was, and still is, vitally interested in the breathing function, particularly as it pertains to playing wind instruments or singing. I remember one occasion when he assembled a group of us, including our first trumpet player, Bud Herseth, Bob Lambert, who was our first trombonist, Jake, and me, and had us all over to the famous pulmonary clinic of the Billings Hospital of the University of Chicago. There he and some of the doctors had set up some elaborate experiments that would not only check our vital capacities, but also the internal pressures built up in the bodies of the players of the four types of brass instruments when played in the various registers and at different dynamic levels. The tests seemed to bear out the fact that when the tuba climbed up into the trombone register and was played at exactly the same dynamic level, when the trombone picked up the note, the pressure inside each player's mouth was identical. This proved true on up into the horn register and then into the trumpet register, always providing that the dynamic level was the same for each player.

Many other fascinating facts were brought out during this session, and I mention this episode as a very good example of Jakes's dedicated search for knowledge which could help all brass players and vocalists. Jake has gone so far as to actually study medicine and physiology to further his own knowledge. He also studied singing, as anyone can tell when they hear his impressive and resonant voice. Over the years he has also collected an impressive array of instruments and machines that can accurately tell him what his students are doing — or not doing, which contributes to his well-deserved title, "The World's Greatest Brass Teacher." Jake would be the first one to object to such an august title, but we who know are fully in agreement that this is quite an accurate evaluation.

I remember one occasion when I was in a prolonged playing slump. I asked for Jake's help and advice to get me out of this depression. He listened to me play for a moment and then advised me, "Phil, stop trying to be so analytical! Shut your eyes and shut off your thinking and just pick up the horn and play it in an instinctive, unthinking manner. Your reflexes will take care of your problem because only a short while ago you were playing well. That ability is still there. In your case analyzing will only make matters worse. You are trying to correct something by thinking about it. In this case it will only tie you up in knots. Play the damned thing like you always have and stop all this negative thinking!" I tried this approach and in two days I was back to normal (for whatever that is worth!). I tell this to illustrate how Jake brings into consideration psychological aspects of playing as well as mechanical and technical aspects. What works for one student certainly will not always work for another. A great teacher realizes this and has the wisdom to know when and when not to use each of these teaching techniques. Jake is the epitome of this kind of teacher.

If this little dissertation seems to be a bit too enthusiastic about my feelings for Arnold Jacobs, you will have to accept it, as there is no other way for me to write about Jake than in superlatives. I still stand by my assertion that Jake is "The World's Greatest Brass Teacher," and I am not in the least bit worried about ever finding someone who will contradict me!

Toby Hanks
Tuba, New York Brass Quintet

Arnold Jacobs is perhaps the most important wind player since J. B. Arban (1825—1889); Arban's organized pedagogy was unprecedented at the time and has been the learning foundation for countless brass players to this day.

Arnold Jacobs' studies and understanding of how the brain and body work together for successful musical performance in the most efficient manner is unprecedented, to my knowledge. These studies are based on one important precept: our bodies are not designed for accurate self-analysis; wind playing or singing (or walking, talking, chewing, etc.) are not controlled directly at a conscious level, and in order to learn how it all works, one must study others, not oneself.

Consequently, Jacobs studied great players and poor players; he read books, talked to specialists in the medical field; examined cadavers (so the legend goes); measured air capacities, air pressures, air flow rates; he studied the muscle systems and how they function in respiration, and so on. This was scientific research in every sense of the word. His understanding of respiration and its function in wind playing and singing (what he is best known for) has demystified the process, and as a result, we have more healthy playing around us today. The tight gut school of breath support that has bound up so many wind players and singers for generations is dying a fast, merciful death.

Less well known, but no less important, are his studies in motor function and conditioned response — how the brain functions to coordinate and control the subtle and complex maneuvers required to play an instrument or sing.

Throughout all of this scientific research, he learned (and never lost sight of the fact) that musical inspiration is the key to fine musical performance. The simpler we can keep our thought processes while performing, the better our bodies can perform. Great players are goal oriented, not procedure oriented. Jacobs learned that scientific understanding is not necessary in order to play well, and it can be a liability if used incorrectly while playing. So, if you don't need to know about it, what good is it? A gifted performer with few difficulties has little or no need for such information. However, many of the most gifted players also become the most active teachers. Their students deserve informed guidance so that they can develop sound physical and mental habits for successful and satisfying progress. Because the gifted player's attempt at self-analysis will be faulty at best, this often creates problems for students where none existed before.

Also, it is well documented that many fine performers develop playing difficulties after many years of success from any number of causes — physical changes caused by aging, loss of teeth, emotional problems, and so on.

After the playing is affected by any of these factors and poor habits reach the unconscious level (conditioned response), a knowledge of the process is vital to be able to rebuild sound procedure from the beginning, replacing poor habits with healthy ones.

Because of the curiosity of Arnold Jacobs we are all more able to develop our skills and those of our students; we are a giant step closer to meeting our potential and are able to trouble shoot problems infinitely more successfully.

His great playing has inspired us, but more important, the knowledge that he has gained and disseminated through his teaching is destined to help future generations of musicians in a way that no one has done since J.B. Arban over 100 years ago.

Ron Hasselman
Trumpet, Minnesota Orchestra

I first met Arnold Jacobs in 1951 while living at the home of Renold Schilke in Evanston, Illinois. As a trumpet student at Northwestern University, I was employed for the summer to paint Schilke's enormous home in order to raise money for my fall tuition. Jake came to Ren's home, along with Frank Crisafulli, Bud Herseth, and Hugh Cowdon, for the purpose of organizing a quintet soon to be named "The Chicago Symphony Brass Quintet," and more immediately to work up a program to perform on a week-long tour throughout Wisconsin.

I wanted to witness this event, so I positioned myself on a ladder by the window of the rehearsal room a full two floors up and over a concrete driveway. An hour and a half later, half painting and half holding dearly onto the ladder, I evidently made the group so nervous about my falling that Jake told Ren to "get that kid off the ladder before he breaks his neck." Ren told me to come in and sit in a corner and listen there if I was that interested. After another hour of rehearsing, they had worked up a solid program with the exception of a grand finale. Ren pulled the Bohme Sextet from his file and set out the music. Hugh asked how they could do a sextet with only five players, and Ren told me to get my trumpet.

The end result was that I was invited along on this tour of Wisconsin as the sixth man of a brass quintet, setting up the stands and music, and joining the quintet on the finale selection.

My fondest recollection of the week was traveling by train up to Northern Wisconsin alone with Jake, as the others went earlier by car. We spent the entire trip in the club car, where Jake discussed brass technique and held me completely spellbound. His concepts and scholarly descriptions were so foreign and above me that I was at a loss to even ask a question for fear of destroying this spell I was under. Little did I realize what a huge impact this man would have on my career and my life. All week long, after every concert, each member of the quintet would give a clinic, and I found myself gravitating to Jake's rather than the trumpet clinics.

I managed to take four lessons with him before I was drafted into the army, where I spent two years traveling around Europe with the Seventh Army Symphony playing principal trumpet.

My first lesson with Jake was a classic. I was asked to play an exercise from page 16 in the Arban book. After a somewhat lengthy explanation of what should be taking place — inspiration, messages via the cerebral cortex, and so on, I played through the exercise again. He then explained more about what didn't take place and what I should do. I began to play again, but was stopped halfway through with more information about the diaphragm, 8th, 9th, and 10th ribs, intercostal muscles, and so on. Once more I began to play. This time I was stopped after the first line for a vital capacity check on the spirometer. I played again, but only up to the fourth bar. "More inspiration, have Herseth in your head. You must have a tape recording in your head of what you want the sound coming out of your horn to be like." I played again, this time only two bars. "More air flow, less breath pressure." Each time I played, the phrases were shorter and shorter until finally only the first note was sounded and I was stopped. One solid hour on one three-line exercise! This came after having studied four years with Schilke and two years with Herseth learning repertoire and style. What an impact, what a blow to my ego, but what a thrill to feel and hear things coming together with ease!

Other memorable moments of my lessons with Jake always include enjoying the deep, rich sound of his voice. On occasion I found myself listening to the quality of his voice rather than the content of his message. I have two tapes of my early lessons, around 1959-60. I've always considered myself to have a bass voice, but listening to the tape, my voice next to his sounds so high-pitched and nasal. In fact, just playing this tape for a few minutes years later, or talking to Jake on the phone and hearing that deep, rich "Hello," would send messages of inspiration and thoughts of air flow through my brain, and my playing would be more relaxed.

Another fond memory of Jake took place about eight years ago in New York. The Minnesota Orchestra was staying in the Wellington Hotel, and the Chicago Symphony was across the street in the Sheraton Hotel. As tradition and hunger have it, many musicians end up in the Carnegie Deli after their concerts, and a few of us from our brass section went there, as did Jake. Several of us were Jacobs' students, but two were not. As Jake is known to do, he began discussing brass techniques, and held a captive audience well past 3:00 a.m. For me it was a recapitulation of many years of study, and it was also fun to watch the newcomers and their all-too-familiar reactions.

I think every one of Jake's students has the address 8839 South Normal and ST 3-5061 imprinted in his memory forever. I can still picture the long trek from my home on the northwest side of Chicago to Jake's home. I never did learn his new phone number when it became all numbers. It was always ST 3.

I also remember his neighborhood well because immediately after my lesson I would drive a block away from his house, park my car, and rehash everything I had learned, profusely writing every thought and recollection from my lesson. Sometimes I would be there almost as long as the lesson itself, trying to relive the past hour, to capture the experience, and remember the stimuli.

As valuable as the lessons were for my playing, it was in the area of teaching that Jake helped me the most. Working with him, I felt the whole process of playing a brass instrument come together. I could now listen to a new student play and have a sensible approach to solving his problems rather than the trial and error method.

I feel, without a doubt, Jake is the foremost Doctor of Brass Playing who ever lived. My first lesson with him was in 1954 and my last (or most recent) was 1979. Over those 25 years I have never ceased to be overwhelmed by both his knowledge and his outstanding musicianship on the tuba.

Merrimon Hipps
Trumpet, Minnesota Orchestra

I first met Arnold Jacobs in 1965, soon after my arrival in Minneapolis. Having grown up in the cultural backwaters of the south, and receiving my education in the south and east, I had never heard of Arnold Jacobs, either as a player or a teacher. The enthusiasm of a number of my colleagues in the Minneapolis Symphony soon convinced me to remedy this shortcoming in my training.

That first lesson was an adventure. As I remember, I took the train, arriving in Chicago at night and staying at the Croydon Hotel. On a scale of one to ten, if the Waldorf was ten, the Croydon was about a minus four. The beds were lumpy, the plumbing undependable, and from the look of some of the female patrons of the bar, there was more for sale there than whiskey sours. The Croydon was the place where traveling orchestras and ballet companies stayed in those days. And it was cheap which, to a guy in his first job at $165 per week (for a 31-week season), was the chief consideration. So, after a restless night and a skimpy breakfast at the coffee shop, I took the Blue Island train to Jacobs' house.

Mrs. Jacobs met me at the door and ushered me into the living room. The rather small house bore evidence of people who read a lot and are reluctant to throw anything away. I suspected there were piles of National Geographics in the attic. In spite of the abundance of books and magazines, I did little reading while I waited. I was nervous, and I was fascinated by the sounds emanating from the basement.

The teaching style with which I was familiar involved playing through prepared etudes followed by comments and suggestions from the teacher — a lot of playing and relatively little talk. What I heard from the basement was obviously different. I couldn't hear the talk, but from the sparsity of musical sounds, I assumed there was a lot of talking going on. Because I knew that many of Mr. Jacobs' students were professionals, I was surprised at the simplicity of the musical material I did hear. No virtuoso etudes, just simple diatonic sequences. "He gets $30 a lesson for this?," I thought (an exorbitant sum to me at that time).

My turn finally came. Mr. Jacobs came upstairs to show the last student out and to greet me. What impressed me most was his voice. To describe it merely as deep and resonant is to do it a disservice. That voice, it seems to me, projects the true essence of the man. It exudes the genuine warmth of his personality, the intensity and brilliance of his mind, the dedication and enthusiasm he feels for his art, and an overwhelming feeling of authority in the best sense of the word. He led me down the narrow stairs, past the usual basement accumulation of debris — the kinds of things you never use, but can't seem to do without — and into his studio.

How can I describe Jacobs' studio? It looked like a mad scientist's laboratory. There were anatomical charts on the walls, and there was the strangest collection of machines, meters, gauges, pipes, and hoses I had ever seen. The centerpiece of this bizarre assemblage was a contraption known to Jacobs' students far and wide as the "Christmas tree." It consisted of a cast-iron base and shaft which appeared to be part of a music stand with a bewildering assortment of dials, tubes, gauges, and hoses.

In looking for material to use to evaluate my playing, Jacobs was dismayed to discover that the first 20 pages were missing from my well-worn Arban book. After instructing me to buy a new Arban, he proceeded to write out Exercise No. 26 from page 16, and asked me to play it legato. When I finished, he complimented my playing as he always did at the start of the lesson — something like, "That sounds very good. I don't know if I can find anything to work on." (The next hour and a half always demonstrated there was plenty to work on.)

What followed was part medical exam, part physiology class, part psychological analysis, and part music lesson. It bore little resemblance to a trumpet lesson as I had come to know it. My vital capacity was measured, the mechanics of my breathing were analyzed in detail with the help of those machines and gauges, and insights into tone production were shared. After a lengthy and erudite monologue, liberally sprinkled with such terms as "intercostal muscles" and "cerebral cortex," he leaned over, looked me in the eye, and said, "Ya dig?"

Two remarkable things became apparent. First, this man had an extraordinary grasp of the technique of tone production and the ability to convey this knowledge with great clarity; second, he was able to put everything into a musical context so that what he taught was not dry technique, it was always a vehicle for musical expression. As I worked to improve my breath control, for instance, I found that I was phrasing more intelligently, paying more attention to the direction of the musical line, and playing with a more vibrant, beautiful sound.

The lesson was open-ended. Instead of trying to cover a specific amount of material in a specific length of time, Jacobs' method was to analyze a problem, introduce a concept to correct the problem, and work until the student had a good grasp of the new concept. This might take an hour or two hours; you simply worked until Mr. Jacobs felt you had the mental tools to work on your own.

I left Chicago that day with that heady mixture of stimulation and fatigue that follows a great learning experience. New concepts, new ways of applying old concepts, and a heightened dedication to learn and grow as a musician: I've never been the same since.

Keith Johnson
Trumpet, North Texas State University

I had heard Arnold Jacobs lecture on several occasions over the years; I had read again and again his now-famous interview in *The Instrumentalist* [reprinted on page 119]. I had held extensive discussions about his teaching with many of his students. Finally, I decided it was time to experience firsthand this man who is in his own lifetime a musical and pedagogical wonder.

I made the required phone call (late on a Sunday night, of course; always the best time to catch him at home), and the lesson was set with his usual admonition to "check again a day or so before the lesson. My schedule often changes at the last minute." Just days before the lesson my wife had unexpected emergency surgery for an exotic, complicated disorder which several doctors tried in vain to explain to me. When I called Arnold Jacobs to tell him I could not keep our appointment, he was most gracious and asked if there were some problem. I told him that my wife had undergone this nearly unpronounceable medical procedure and he said, "Oh, yes, that's a condition wherein . . . etc." It was the most direct, lucid, and sensible explanation of her condition I had heard to date. I thought at the time that anyone who could explain an involved medical situation with such directness and clarity could surely both understand and express the essentials as well as the subtleties of brass performance.

My conclusion was borne out during the lessons I took in the years that followed. What Arnold Jacobs also proved was that he was as unpredictable as he was brilliant. I had long heard of his reputation for working with pressure gauges, respirometers, and air bags; about his use of hoses and breathing tubes; and, of course, about buzzing the mouthpiece. He did have me play on the mouthpiece — exuberantly, extensively, and, above all, musically — but none of the other things was ever mentioned.

What he did talk about, however, was embouchure, articulation, problems peculiar to the piccolo trumpet (that anyone who hasn't played piccolo could know so much is both surprising and a bit maddening!), upper register, dealing with conductors, listening skills, performance anxiety, a simple but vigorous approach to respiration, and always and paramount, making beautiful music.

At the end of each lesson I would sit down just outside the studio and write down everything I could recall that he had said. As I look back over those notes the range of topics continues to amaze me; he covered everything from the interpretation of Arutunian's *Trumpet Concerto* to physical preparation for the high trumpet part in the *B Minor Mass*; from something as simple as good posture to something as complex as how the neuromuscular system translates thoughts into physical responses. He always had the same *idée fixe*: think music, think music, think music. "Don't ask questions. Make statements." "Hear Herseth playing that phrase." "Sing, sing!" "More vibrato, warmer," and on and on.

Many people have bemoaned the fact that Arnold Jacobs has never written down his ideas in an extensive format. It is true that we would all surely benefit if he does ever undertake such a creation, but as one who has written at some length on brass playing, I have doubts as to whether Arnold Jacobs' ideas would have the same impact in writing. It is not because his ideas are erroneous or because he lacks skill with words. His factual knowledge of brass performance is possibly without equal. Yet the validity of an idea often lives or dies by the medium in which it is transmitted; and as anyone who has had a lesson with Arnold Jacobs will testify, there is no other experience quite like it. In that terribly personal, at times excruciatingly intense one-to-one crucible, he transmits ideas into the student, judges their appropriateness, and enables the player to transcend old limits and achieve new levels of excellence. His uncompromising standards, his insistence on only the best one can deliver, and his complete devotion to the art of making music are so intertwined with his specific ideas that the best writing could only convey a partial impact. It is not just what he says but rather how he somehow enables each player to produce music from his deepest resources. He shows the performer how to unleash a reservoir of ability, and the result is frequently as unsettling as it is rewarding. I have rarely played better than when he showed me how much I was capable of producing, and I never left a lesson without feeling a satisfied kind of exhaustion.

All of us, his students and ours, are in his debt. He is a rare breed, and it is not likely we shall see his equal again in our lifetimes.

Fritz Kaenzig
Tuba, University of Illinois

After two years of study with Robert LeBlanc at Ohio State University, he suggested I call Mr. Jacobs during the upcoming summer and try to begin study with him. Mr. LeBlanc had studied with Mr. Jacobs during his graduate work at Eastman and felt I would benefit at this point in my development by taking some lessons with the master of respiratory function in wind playing. I had listened to recordings of the Chicago Symphony under Fritz Reiner while growing up, so Arnold Jacobs had become something of a hero to me. His beautiful, rich, resonant sound and distinctive style of phrasing became the standard by which I measured good tuba playing. So it was with a good deal of trepidation that I dialed the telephone number of this great man from my home in Dayton.

The resonance and depth of his voice over the phone nearly matched his tuba sound and did little to dispel my nervousness. I managed to quell the shakes enough to blurt out my reason for calling and after several more calls and a couple of months, I was on my way to his house on South Normal Avenue in Chicago. My preconceptions about a mansion with manicured lawns and a long driveway with an iron grill emblazoned with the initials A.J. were soon shattered. Could there be another South Normal Avenue? Surely the great Mr. Jacobs didn't live in a lower middle-class section of town! When reality could no longer be denied, I entered the walk through the thick bushes on either side of his house. Mrs. Jacobs kindly greeted me and showed me the way into the living room through a healthy collection of newspapers, magazines, and books. Mrs. Jacobs' mother kept me company in the living room by telling me stories about their cat. I might have thought I was in the wrong house, except for the sounds of a tuba lesson being conducted in the basement. I still thought that perhaps Mr. Jacobs might be dressed in the splendor of a tuxedo, but nothing could have been further from the truth.

My first glimpse of Arnold Jacobs was of a rather rotund gentleman dressed in baggy pants held up by suspenders and a shirt not quite as generous as his girth. Then he spoke in that beautiful bass voice and proceeded to lead me through his low-ceilinged basement to a room nearly as magnificent as the man himself; machines and tubas filled the room. He caught me off-guard by asking the purpose of this first lesson with him. I replied quickly, "Breathing," and was nearly speechless when he asked, "What else?" I stammered something about needing help with my low range, so he chose to start there. "About how much time do you spend daily in the lower register?" he asked. "You mean every day?" I responded. After starting at a figure of 30 minutes, I was down to "maybe five minutes on the low range alone" by the end of his several hmmm's. When I reached my final figure, he finally ended my misery by stating, "I thought that lack of practice in that register might be the problem. Now let's move on to the respiratory function." He then gave me a lesson that kept me thinking conceptually and working to achieve those concepts for most of the next school year.

I continued to study with Mr. Jacobs semi-regularly for the next several years and continue to this day. At first my lessons were undertaken solely for my own performance improvement. Since entering the teaching profession at the University of Wisconsin-Madison, my lessons have often been filled with questions designed to help me correct the problems my students encounter. He has helped me to keep from giving into students' desires to talk about problems in terms of embouchure fixes and to refute adamant emphasis on diaphragmatic support by explaining anatomy (often with charts) and the body's physical responses to specific conceptual commands. He has helped to get me away from performing and teaching from an approach based on psychomotor responses and has substituted concepts of song and wind in their place. He has hooked me up to machines to measure my lung capacity, drawn lines on my music to show movements of air and thicknesses of vibrating membranes, and helped with outside stimuli to show me that forced air doesn't necessarily produce a louder sound than relaxed, projected wind. This latter axiom was demonstrated to me by having me blow with mouthpiece alone into a funnel connected by a tube to a decibel meter. After blowing as loud and hard as possible, I managed about a six on the meter. Then Mr. Jacobs effortlessly blew a rich, full buzz (with mouthpiece) into the same funnel and produced a ten.

Arnold Jacobs' psychology of teaching is so effective with individuals that they have often attempted to imitate his style. His model is well worth emulating. He teaches with great energy and commitment in each lesson, seldom showing any signs of weariness once a lesson begins, touching students to keep their full attention or to emphasize a point, expecting the most detailed imitation of sounds, the finest production of tone a student can muster with his mind and wind, and never wavering from his approach of song and wind. He is not dogmatic to the extent that all lessons are the same. He will change the stimuli to achieve a desired product, even temporarily contradicting what he may have told another student, for each student that enters Mr. Jacobs' studio in The Fine Arts Building on Michigan Avenue is an individual with unique needs and abilities. It is the mark of his masterful teaching that he is able to meld his teaching media to fit individuals' needs and to say what a student needs to hear to effect change. Mr. Jacobs' emphasis on simple demands based on the beauty of sound and thoughtful phrasing coupled with the movement of wind is such that at times you can walk out of his studio wondering why you were not making music these ways already. Then those simple commands keep haunting you until they are second nature: more vowel in the sound in all registers, more air across the lips for the vibrating membrane to operate properly, collapse the stomach and chest naturally to expel wind, concentrate on artistic sound and pitch before ever playing a note, more fundamental in the sound, and so on. The inner rhythm and phrasing that Mr. Jacobs teaches is always evident in his recorded and live performances with the Chicago Symphony Orchestra. He sets the highest levels of performance for all to hear and sometimes treats students to these same performance levels by performing for us in lessons. What a glorious musician to hear and to try and imitate.

Recently, I had the opportunity to hear him play in the C.S.O. in a Bruckner 6th Symphony under Kubelik's baton. When Mr. Jacobs came on stage to warm up I thought that he had finally lost his performance abilities; he was warming up with a paltry tone barely audible. He had obviously done enough warm-up elsewhere that day, because the first entrance of full brass was evidence that Mr. Jacobs had lost none of his sound and artistry.

After 50 years of teaching and performing, Mr. Jacobs has lost none of his enthusiasm and commitment to his art and profession. Nor will he at some point in the future, for there is no fraudulent front to this man and musician. His masterful legacy will remain as long as there are tubists, brass players, and musicians.

41

Robert Allen Karon
Trumpet, Los Angeles Brass

Arnold Jacobs has had a deep and far-reaching influence on my career and personal life. Not a day goes by that his teachings don't affect me in some way. In fact, I don't believe that I would still be playing now, or be married, or be a father, or be as happy if it were not for Jake.

There are many facets to my relationship with Arnold. There are the lessons and how they have changed over the years; there are the studies I've had with his former students; there is the effect on my career; and finally, there are the extra-musical benefits.

My first lesson took place in the summer of 1976. I had just completed three years of paying my dues in the Maracaibo Symphony in Venezuela. My playing then was not very happy or satisfying; there was too much nervousness and discomfort in my performance. To make this even worse, colleagues had preyed upon my lack of confidence unmercifully; I was full of doubts and anger.

One afternoon in Los Angeles I was visiting Tony Plog who had a guest staying over from Las Vegas. In our conversation this fellow mentioned that he had taken a few lessons from Jacobs and that it had really helped his breathing and confidence. Breathing, I thought, was my problem; I never seemed to have enough air. I was looking for a couple of exercises to be the cure-all, a magic formula. From Juilliard days I remembered seeing Bob Gillespe doing Jacobs' breathing exercises. He had a huge, confident sound, so I wrote to Arnold Jacobs and eventually called for a lesson. I had decided to return to New York City to work and arranged to stay with Phil Smith in Chicago on the way there.

The first lesson was mind-boggling. Jacobs had me inhaling and exhaling through all sorts of machines; he spoke of "wind and song," and eventually when I would hyperventilate, we would talk. He was concerned that I had a lot of wheezing and presented the possibility that I may have had a medical condition. He gave me a five-liter anesthesia bag to use in my practice. I went back to Phil's exhausted and somewhat confused. There were so many thoughts running through my head. I called home, anxious about this possi-

42

ble respiratory condition and considered returning to California. A day went by. I wrote notes about the lesson, practiced on the bag, and played duets and excerpts with Phil until his wife couldn't stand it any longer.

At the next lesson things started to click. There was less wheezing. I was just fighting myself too much and instead of breathing I was squeezing. Moreover, when Jake looked at me, said I was a fine player and that it was "okay to go ahead, don't be afraid, make mistakes," for the first time I felt relaxed and secure, and began to rebuild some self-esteem. There is a real exhilaration when you've played something to his satisfaction and he clasps his hands together in triumph!

I had one more lesson that week. After each one I was exhausted and had pages of notes. When I made my way to New York, I was supercharged with new habits to form. A little later I had an audition for the Emerson, Lake, and Palmer orchestra and got the job using borrowed instruments. Jake's ideas had worked.

Over the last eight years I have been finding ways to stop in Chicago a couple times each year on my way to and from New York, Los Angeles, Mexico City, and on road tours. (No wonder he always asks where I'm calling from.) I've stayed with many different friends for as little as a day to as long as several months at a time. Many of those non-lesson days were long and lonely. Sometimes I stayed quite a way out of town, and the commute by train for each lesson was an odyssey, but it was worthwhile.

I think that over the years the emphasis in Jake's method of teaching has shifted somewhat. Of course, at first there was so much to get going. He started by using various meters and gauges, demonstrated good posture, breathing exercises, and correct use of the tongue through speech. Many of these ideas had been presented to me by previous teachers, but his explanations and images somehow made more sense. Usually I was able to imitate the correct approach in a matter of minutes. Certainly his investigations into physiological and psychological aspects of brass playing added depth to these explanations. However, I think his success in teaching also has a lot to do with his natural ability to focus in on each individual's thought patterns and experiences and to relate on a personal level.

When my head was spinning from all of the deep breathing, Jacobs would tell me to forget the clinical analysis and become an artist projecting the image of a great trumpet sound from my mind.

I've had many teachers tell me to "think," "think before you stink," "get into the music," and "engage brain before playing," but no image ever hit home like the one Jake made. He had me imagine what Herseth would sound like on the opening to "Pictures" before I played it. As a result, I sounded better than ever on that passage. Then he asked me to repeat the same passage, this time concentrating on a Cubs game. Nothing came out of the horn! That might not be saying too much about the Chicago Cubs, but it says it all about playing the trumpet. "There are two horns," he insists, "the one in your hand and the one in your head. The one in your hand only reflects what the one in your head is doing. It's like the player piano roll to the keyboard." In the early lessons that was not easy for me to do, but as the years went by and the new, good habits became predominant, (I practice the mechanics religiously every day, almost 3000 repetitions by now), he shifted the emphasis to the musical ideas and imagery. Certainly we would focus on a specific aspect of the wind, tongue, or embouchure, but in general the main consideration became the ultimate product, the sound of the music.

I have also studied with two of his former students. In 1965, when I was a sophomore in high school, I studied with the Principal Trumpet of the Minneapolis Symphony, Stephen Chenette. It wasn't until later that I realized Chenette had studied with Jacobs. He was quite involved with techniques and he had much of the apparatus that I later recognized at Jake's studio; apparently Jacobs was working extensively with Steve on breathing because he had an exceptionally large lung capacity. I was only in Minneapolis for one year, and perhaps I was too young to understand what was being presented to me, but the desire to achieve those goals, the solfege, the breathing, the posture, and the sound, remained in the back of my mind.

Much later, when I was in New York, I had the pleasure of studying with Vincent Penzarella, one of Jacobs' most famous cases. Vince worked on technique, but he was also deeply involved with the spirit of the music. Apparently, it was the music, specifically "Ave Maria," that triggered Vince's ability to play after an injury. Naturally, that experience is reflected in his enthusiasm for the sound of the music and its emotion. Steve and Vince were contemporaries at The Curtis Institute of Music; they both studied with Arnold Jacobs, yet received unique, tailor-made instruction, which they have generously imparted to their students. Perhaps in years past, when Jacobs was developing his methodology of breathing techniques, he was more technical in his teaching. Now I think he has found a simplicity of explanation that triggers complicated motor responses. Musical thoughts head the list of those simple ideas. Nonetheless, Jacobs has all of these resources at his disposal and combines both the technical and musical aspects of teaching to suit each player and his problem. This talent and insight makes him a truly unique teacher.

For me, there would be no career in music if it weren't for Arnold Jacobs' guidance. The E.L.P. audition was only one instance. Years later I auditioned for Second Trumpet in the Sacramento Symphony. This was after I had left Mexico City, again a time when my self-esteem was low. The audition was a failure, and I didn't even make the finals. I decided to go to Chicago to see Jacobs for a few lessons. On my return I took the Sacramento audition for Principal Trumpet and won. That entire year was heavily influenced by Jacobs. Even when my chops were sore from overuse and abuse, the breathing, musical thoughts, and renewed confidence from our telephone conversations saw me through. Yet what I have learned from Arnold goes much further than the breathing and other techniques, and further than the ability to project sound images based on the musical score. He also gave me some very good advice when he suggested that I take the chance to freelance in Los Angeles rather than remain in Sacramento. He even suggested that I get my girlfriend in Sacramento pregnant to assure her coming to L.A. with me. When I explained that she was a nurse, he realized that perhaps that wouldn't work. Nonetheless, she did marry me, and a year after moving to Los Angeles, our son was born. I am very happy with my life here. Jake's advice was good, and the confidence he gave me has allowed me to really enjoy it.

Arnold Jacobs has a happy, positive, and cheerful attitude about life and music. It emanates from him and he has enhanced my life both musically and personally. Arnold Jacobs is more than a great teacher; he is a great friend.

Arnold Jacobs, taken by Paul Walton

James E. Kowalsky
Trumpet, Formerly University of Alaska

My first exposure to Arnold Jacobs and other brass performers of the Chicago Symphony Orchestra came during the spring of 1953. As a senior in high school in eastern Wisconsin I traveled 30 miles one way with our high school band to Green Bay to hear an afternoon concert by the Chicago Symphony Brass Quintet.

That experience captured my imagination. I knew upon hearing the first phrases of the Quintet's performance that I surely must be hearing performers who were unexcelled.

I clearly recall the smooth buoyant style of execution of Arnold Jacobs' tuba playing. Equally striking was the clarity, the smoothness, the ease of performance and the sweet sound of Adolph Herseth. These were hallmarks of the ensemble, and I recognized that I was hearing something which for me was unique. Traveling home that evening, in awe, I knew there could be few others who sounded that way. I knew too that I had to hear these people again. I was puzzled by flawless, superb performance on the one hand, that was also powerful and moving, even to my uninitiated ear. The effort they seemed to expend appeared minimal if even discernible. I had difficulty understanding this. Were these people real? Did they relate to people such as me? Could I ever approach them? What did they do to perform this way?

I played the trumpet during high school with a naturalness that seemed to disappear during my early years at college. I became filled with doubt, self-conscious about my playing, and apparently began down a long road of decline or bare maintenance of performance; bad habits entered into my entire approach to performance. I would force the sound, trying to produce the tone with tense abdominal musculature.

I now realize that I was in a situation needing expert teaching of a remedial nature. Why had it not occurred to me at that time to seek out a teacher with known, demonstrated abilities to take performers in need of remedial work? To this day I'm not certain why I didn't seek out Arnold Jacobs for help from the beginning. I do not think I knew of him as a teacher in those years. I may have had the notion carried with me from hearing him in 1953 that someone of that stature would have little interest in teaching someone such as me.

47

I lacked the range, the confidence that comes with it, and the ease of production. I often experimented, trying to fix things, tightening stomach muscles into a firm, hard ball and then forcing the upper notes. These were unknowing, ill-informed directions; but these were techniques I had been taught by teachers, or ideas about performance which I had picked up from them. Much of this anguished experimentation took place while I taught public school music in small communities near Madison, Wisconsin.

It surprises me that during these same years, I had managed to attend Chicago Symphony Orchestra concerts regularly in Milwaukee, but it had not occurred to me that the very teacher who could offer the correct guidance was sitting right there making such exciting music in the brass section of the CSO (these were the Fritz Reiner years). It had not occurred to me that Arnold Jacobs might be available for teaching had I only asked. No one at that point even offered that advice to me, and I did hang out with quite a few active brass performers among other musicians.

I went back to graduate school at the University of Wisconsin, Madison after teaching in the nearby public schools from 1957-1962. Just before enrolling, my friend Don Heeren finally stepped in to help me change directions.

As a student of Arnold Jacobs, Don encouraged me to take the big step and go to Arnold. Don convinced me that Jake would help in ways that I would never be able to imagine or to comprehend unless I got down there into his basement studio. I agreed. I started driving weekends to Chicago and took a lesson approximately every other Saturday. I drove round trip about 385 miles.

My first lessons were extraordinary I thought, and very basic. Myths were crushed, one after another. Using material in *Arban*, he proceeded to illustrate to me, and to have me illustrate in turn, elementary concepts:

- the importance of becoming acquainted with the sound and the sensation of breath while breathing in through the mouth (the sound of "Oh", and a coolness on the back of the windpipe)

- becoming acquainted with breath as motion while blowing simple phrases in slur, mid range

- performing the phrase on the mouthpiece alone with good pitch, style, and tone color, then repeating it on the instrument immediately, before losing the thought of playing it without the

48

aid of the trumpet. The trumpet is nothing more than a loud-speaker: you create the sound, the style, and the pitch change at the mouthpiece and never with the valves of the trumpet

- guiding the lower rib and thus entire ribcage upward using the palms of the hand while inspirating the air — and allowing the shoulders to rise (rising as a result, not the cause, of taking a full breath)

- using the spirometer as a visual aid (challenge yourself visually to reach a certain mark breathing in), thence to the trumpet and simple phrase immediately

- improvising the breathing bag from plastic, a coathanger, and a cardboard toilet paper core for mouthpiece.

- using the visual column to blow a metal ball upward to a certain number and holding it there with the breath and the visual measurement while he held his thumb over a hole to cover it along the thin plastic air tube connected to the column — then to gradually remove his thumb to uncover the hole and allow the air to escape, but asking me to try — through rapid blowing now, to try to maintain the ball at the same mark as before, thus allowing me to illustrate to myself the dramatic difference between static air, and moving air, or breath as motion — and then going immediately to the trumpet for more simple material in slur (teaching you to intervene in your psychology)

- constant urging to think of the air as a bow on a stringed instrument, always moving but not pressing down too hard (the breath as a full bow)

- differentiating between breath flow and breath pressure by pencil graph illustration at the top of the page of music

- transferring the sound from one note upward to the next

- imagining the sound of the trumpet in the mind while playing the phrase

Notwithstanding the ingenious methods Arnold used to normalize my breathing, his greatest contribution was his ability to convince me that all those physiological functions are triggered responses, brought into play by the player who thinks of the musical phrase, who "mentalizes" the end result. Even in warm-up he would admonish that warming up is not training muscles or really doing anything with muscles, as brass players are so commonly taught; rather, the warm-up is putting into being the very best sounds as you remember them from the day before — the recreation of one's finest sounds.

He used countless examples throughout my lessons to stimulate me to bring about playing through conceptualizing the sound, color, style, and phrases. I've heard him illustrate this to others as well. I recall one summer in a Gunnison, Colorado music camp tuba class in which he used one student to illustrate these concepts to others. The student played a phrase from the start to the finish as best he could. Then Arnold, sitting with him in front of the class, started the phrase and the student took over at a preappointed measure, imagining that he was in fact the same performer and was continuing the same sound. The difference was substantial from the first attempt, and it was immediate.

Arnold would tell me that we correct bad habits by forming new ones, not by trying to get rid of the old ones. Going to the practice room with the goal of isolating a bad habit is merely to continue it. Rather, he would admonish, the way to get it out of your system is to learn a new habit; bad habits are extinguished by being supplanted with new ones.

Throughout my two and a half years of study with Arnold, I continued to be fascinated and perplexed at how some performers could play so effortlessly and naturally as we like to think of it. One Friday Arnold and I rode in to the concert from his home that noon hour on the train. I dwelled on this and other matters with him as we jounced along in that old musty rail car and he left me with a thought I haven't forgotten. "In other words," he said after going through one of his lengthy but profound enough explanations, "all you have to do is imagine that you are a natural player long enough, and you will become one." On the one hand, an oversimplification, but on the other, a marvelous encouragement of how to approach performance as a musician. Notwithstanding the breathing aids and all that emphasis, I felt that his advice to me that Friday noon was also a pretty fair summation of the substance of his teaching.

David Langlitz
Principal Trombone
Metropolitan Opera Orchestra

The first time I heard the name Arnold Jacobs I was a 17-year-old high school student. All during that year I would travel on Saturday from Albany to New York City to take trombone lessons with a member of the Metropolitan Opera Orchestra, who had studied with Arnold Jacobs during his student years. My teacher patiently spent hours working with me on breathing. He augmented these lessons by giving me mental exercises to do, such as having me create a musical phrase in my mind and then imitating it as precisely as possible on the trombone. These breathing and mental exercises always seemed to produce the most rapid and lasting improvement in my playing, and were credited by my teacher to Arnold Jacobs. At that point I decided that some day I would study with this man in Chicago who had made such an important contribution to my musical growth.

As a student at Juilliard I often noticed that many of the brass players whose playing I respected had studied with Jacobs. All roads seemed to be leading to Chicago, so I scraped together what little money I had, borrowed a car, and drove there. The day before I met Jacobs I had scheduled a lesson with Ed Kleinhammer. I distinctly remember the phrase he used to describe his colleague and friend. He said, "Arnold Jacobs is not only a great musician, he is also a great man." The following day I took my first lesson with Arnold Jacobs and began a relationship that has lasted 15 years.

Recently a book on physics has been published called *The Dancing Wu Li Masters* by Gary Zukov. In the first chapter the author defines what a master is: someone who "teaches essence; when the essence is perceived he teaches what is necessary to expand the perception." Arnold Jacobs is the embodiment of that essence. While many other teachers are content to dance around the periphery of the essentials of musicianship, Jacobs goes directly to its source. Once the student has grasped the essentials, the details of correct physical functioning have an uncanny knack of falling into place. After the musical concept is formed, the mind then directs the body to respond appropriately. This concept is directly opposed to the more common and sterile approach to teaching in which a student struggles to play correctly by following a prescribed set of rules for embouchure, articulation, etude work, and so on. Jacobs' approach to brass playing demands sensitivity, imagination, and intuition. With him the music is the message, and it is of the highest importance.

I chose to adopt this particular approach in teaching because it works outrageously well. If a student is having a difficult time, I will often give him some of Jacobs' breathing exercises. Next I'll have him close his eyes and imagine the problem passage being performed by what he considers to be an outstanding trombonist. I instruct him to hear the sound, phrasing, and articulation clearly in his mind. When he picks up his horn and imitates what he just heard in his mind, it inevitably sounds much better — often to the student's amazement.

In 1974 there was a trombone vacancy with the Metropolitan Opera Orchestra. I decided to take the audition six days before the preliminaries. Because of my inexperience with the opera repertoire there were several excerpts required for the audition that I didn't know, including *Wozzeck* and *Othello*. During those six days before the audition I practiced every excerpt in my mind as often as possible, and Arnold Jacobs' words were my constant companions:

"How good is your imagination? Create the sound in your mind
    and then imitate what you've just heard."
"Wind and Song."
"Don't get caught in the mechanics of the instrument; what's
    needed is a childlike simplicity."
"Be a musical storyteller and psychologically project beyond the
    instrument."
"Challenge yourself to great artistry with every note you play."

A teacher can never force a student to become a great musician. I am convinced a great teacher is one who allows the student to realize the potential within himself. The greatest musical contribution Arnold Jacobs made to my life was convincing me that my greatest teacher was my own imagination, that what makes an artist great is his thinking, and that you eventually begin to sound like your own concept. He taught me that I could attain the expertise of the great brass players with the use of my own imagination and intuition as guides.

During the 1984-85 season I took a one-year leave of absence from the Metropolitan Opera Orchestra to accept a Fulbright Performing Artist Award to the Orient. During this year I played with orchestras and gave solo performances and master classes in Japan, Korea, and the People's Republic of China. Foremost in my teaching are these ideas that have worked so successfully for so many students. It appears that the influence of Arnold Jacobs will continue to contribute to brass players throughout the world. The vehicle will be the many fine performers and teachers that have graduated from his studio.

Because of his brilliance, I have often felt Arnold Jacobs would have been equally successful in whatever career he attempted: music, medicine, science, or psychology. However, the most profound contribution he has made to my life goes beyond the music studio. His intelligence, humor, integrity, and kindness as a man and artist have contributed to my life greatly, and my existence has been enormously enriched and nurtured by my relationship with this great man.

Mark H. Lawrence
Principal Trombone, San Francisco Symphony

I had my first experience with Arnold Jacobs when I was 30 years old and had been Principal Trombonist with the San Francisco Symphony for five years. When I walked into his office feeling like a teenager again, he immediately put me at ease with his reassuring manner. Although I only had three lessons with Mr. Jacobs, I received enough food for thought to last a long time.

The single most unifying concept he imparted to me was "thinking of the end product, not the process involved in achieving that product," for example, thinking of how you want something to sound, not what you have to do to get it to sound that way. His use of imagery was marvelous, and he opened my eyes to a whole new thought process.

Most of what he said was aimed at steering students away from trying to control their bodily functions while they play. "Let the brain be occupied with beautiful sounds and music making, and allow the body to do what it has to do to achieve these ends without interference." To underscore this philosophy he used phrases such as: "Feed the piano roll, not the keys," "Think of the sound, not how it feels," "When you breathe you're at a gas station, when you exhale you're an artist," "Think of the lips as vocal chords," "Conceive the sound in the head," "Sing when you play," "When warming up, try to play as beautifully as possible," and "When playing, make a statement, don't ask a question."

At first I was a bit overwhelmed by the vast amount of information I was receiving, but little by little I was able to utilize it in my daily playing and teaching with very favorable results. Mr. Jacobs' approach is extremely valuable because true ease and efficiency in playing cannot be achieved until the body is able to perform in a natural way without interference from the brain. I feel extremely fortunate to have had the benefit of Mr. Jacobs' expertise, and I hope I can impart to my students a small part of what he gave to me.

Daniel Perantoni
Professor of Music, Arizona State University

I first met Arnold Jacobs (Jake, as many of his colleagues and students fondly call him), when he was on tour with the Chicago Symphony Orchestra at the University of Illinois in Champaign-Urbana, Illinois. I was about two months into my new career as an instructor of music at the University of Illinois. I met Jake backstage and invited him to my home for some refreshments. He graciously accepted, which turned out to be the beginning of a lasting relationship with him as my teacher and friend. He was so open and sincere that my wife and I felt we had already known him for years. The conversation obviously led to the tuba, concepts of teaching, and so on. I was amazed by the amount of knowledge he readily expounded and his command of the English language. I never told him that one of my reasons for coming to Illinois was to have the opportunity to study with him. Shortly after this meeting I began my many trips to Chicago for the most beneficial study of my life.

Jake introduced me to the many medical devices relating to inhalation and exhalation, which helped relieve the physical stress and tension that I had been using. I have met many people who have had one or two lessons with him and are under the impression that his only direction is working on breathing. This is far from the truth. I can still hear him say, "Dan, all this information dwelling on the physical is useless to you as a player unless your main goal is to make music. Good physical habits must be developed as a conditional response free of unnecessary tension. You must have the message in your mind. The end result is the important issue."

There are many gifted composers at the University of Illinois, and during the late 60s and early 70s I studied and performed a great deal of new music. When I performed an avant-garde solo in one of my lessons Jake offered some valuable comments and was interested in the expansion of the tuba literature. Because of my interest in chamber and solo playing he encouraged me to purchase an F tuba. I took his advice immediately, and this proved to be the major turning point in my success as a player. The experience I gained from playing the CC and the F tubas strengthened my accuracy, clarity, and overall sound on both instruments. Jake also encouraged me to experiment with different mouthpieces and other equipment. He has a large collection of various instruments available at his studio, and I always feel like a boy in a candy shop when I visit him.

Robert Tucci, another student of Jake's, and I met years ago and decided we had many common interests. Bob is presently living in Munich and performs with the Bavarian State Opera. Jake encouraged us to get involved with Fred Marrich at Custom Music Company for consultation in upgrading his products. We felt that the tuba had been neglected in quality and development, especially in this country; over the years, we have tried to offer tubists more variety when choosing an instrument. Most tubists who have listened to Jake would have loved to get their hands on one of the two large bore York tubas he owns. To my knowledge these were the only two ever made. Bob and I felt that this sound should be preserved, and we were committed to encourage someone to make such an instrument. However, to do this properly, the tuba had to be made mostly by hand, the same way the originals were constructed in the late 1920s and early 30s. We finally convinced Peter Hirsbrunner, a quality craftsman and engineer from Sumiswald, Switzerland, to undertake this project. Jake loaned me one of the two York tubas; I sent it to Peter in Switzerland for measurement, but the instrument arrived badly damaged. The bell was almost beyond repair. Peter, Bob, and I were sick! I dreaded having to tell Jake. When I had the courage to tell him, he was calm as always. Fortunately, with Peter's expertise, the instrument was completely overhauled and returned to Jake like new. The process took about a year; during that time Jake was patient and understanding while the rest of us were nervous wrecks.

After owning the Hirsbrunner copy I discovered that Jake's concept of teaching is directly related to the way this tuba responds. The instrument demands the player to be very efficient. It just will not respond, particularly in the low register, when playing with unnecessary body tension. When I concentrated on moving a large volume of air under less intensity, the tuba seemed to play itself.

With Jake's many musical interests I was not surprised to learn of his love for jazz. He told me that early in his career he used to play string bass and tuba in different jazz settings. I learned that he loved to listen to good jazz and he encouraged me to send him recordings. When visiting his new home I remember asking if he had a stereo. He said that he bought a new one years ago, but didn't get around to unpacking the original carton. He really is not as organized in outside tasks as he is in his teaching and performance. Frankly, he never takes much time from his heavy teaching and performing schedule.

Arnold Jacobs continues to be an important influence on me both personally and professionally. His outlook on life is always positive no matter how difficult the situation might be. His love for his profession is unsurpassed. His concept of teaching has been a revelation. I feel fortunate to have had the opportunity to study with the ultimate teacher. When I think of Jake, I see that ever-smiling face.

Marvin Chapman Perry II
Principal Trumpet, Indianapolis Symphony Orchestra

Through the years I heard several colleagues of mine mention that Arnold Jacobs was a very fine teacher. During one season with the Indianapolis Symphony Orchestra, I gave a solo trumpet recital that should have gone better than it did, considering the amount of work that went into it. Because I lived less than 200 miles from Chicago, I decided it was time to take advantage of some of the brass expertise in that city, so I contacted Mr. Jacobs.

I had my first lessons with Mr. Jacobs because I was having some problems related to breathing at the time, and with the physical adjustments I was making. His emphasis was always on mental music making; this is the key that has helped me survive the adjustments, some of which I am still incorporating into my playing. His emphasis on the music has helped me in my preparation of pieces immensely, and is contrary to any previous teaching I had where the emphasis was on learning the fingers and then letting the music follow. Now the emphasis is on learning. After I know what I want to do with the music, the fingerings and other physical aspects follow more easily and naturally. More than any other aspect of Jacobs' teaching this has affected the whole psychology of my performance and teaching despite some of my own physical difficulties which he has also helped me with.

I cannot recall another teacher who has zeroed in on my thinking, or not thinking, while playing my instrument; Jacobs knows when a performer doesn't quite have the entire musical grasp of a passage. One case in point is the Hummel Concerto in E for trumpet and orchestra. After working on the Hummel trumpet concerto and performing it since high school, I was having difficulty with playing several passages consistently when I was preparing it to play with the Indianapolis Symphony Orchestra. The opportunity to solo with the orchestra came on rather short notice, and fortunately, Mr. Jacobs agreed to help me with the piece. He made the weak areas of my preparation clear to me, and he was helpful in demonstrating what I needed to do before playing the piece with the orchestra (the performance went extremely well). After this, with a lesson on how to prepare for a performance, deciding what to do with every single note, I realized more mental discipline was necessary in all of my musical preparations. I'm convinced that good performances are not the result of good luck, but of a disciplined mental approach as well as physical practice. The sloppy playing that comes out of my instrument and those of my co-workers is the result of sloppy thinking or not thinking.

I admit I have some physical difficulties, particularly involving the inadequate use of my lungs. Even in my first lesson with Mr. Jacobs, I was amazed at how much my sound improved when I loosened up my breathing. He immediately started me on some exercises to help use all of my breath capacity, instead of about 75 percent of it. Of course, using more air affected other areas of my playing. Although it takes time to replace habits formed during 20 years of playing, playing the trumpet now takes less physical effort than it did five years ago; the results are obvious to my colleagues, too.

Once I called Mr. Jacobs because I had cracked a rib; it wasn't a serious fracture, but I had to wear a brace, which hampered my breathing. In Indianapolis, we don't have a big trumpet section or even a contracted assistant, so it was a serious situation, especially with the prospect of having to wear the brace for almost two months. In this situation Mr. Jacobs showed me how much pressure I was using as I played up high, especially on piccolo trumpet. It taught me about why I would see spots all too frequently when playing high register passages. What I learned from him at that lesson enabled me to play all rehearsals and performances of the Bach "B-Minor Mass" five months later. I did not see any spots during that whole time — a first for me.

Mr. Jacobs also helped me with several areas of my playing including embouchure, posture, and the psychology of good performing. Everything I have learned from him has increased my enjoyment of what I do as a performer and teacher.

Harvey Phillips
Professor of Tuba, Indiana University

I have enjoyed my association with Arnold Jacobs since I first met him in August 1950. We first became acquainted when I was about to leave my position with the Ringling Bros. and Barnum & Bailey Circus Band to accept an invitation from William Bell in New York City for private study with him at the Juilliard School of Music. I called Mr. Jacobs from Los Angeles to inquire if he could recommend someone to replace me in the circus band. He recommended one of his young tuba students, Harold McDonald, who joined the Pittsburgh Symphony Orchestra in 1952 and remained there until his retirement in 1981.

After arriving in New York City, getting settled as a student and established as a free-lance player, I often worked with musicians who spoke to me about Arnold Jacobs. They always spoke with great respect, admiration, and affection for him. I was deeply impressed, for I admired each of these musicians as extraordinary artists on their respective instruments. As William Bell did, they were kind enough to take me under their wings; from them I learned much about our profession and making music. These artists' boundless admiration for Arnold Jacobs as a performer and teacher inspired me to improve my own performance so that one day I might earn that same level of respect. In private lessons and in conversations with William Bell, I was continually impressed by his references to Arnold Jacobs. So, while I never actually studied with Arnold Jacobs, I learned very early in my career about his incredible artistry as a performer and about the respect great musicians had for his knowledge and unique pre-eminence as a teacher.

Over the years, since 1950, I have been privileged to have numerous opportunities for contact and association with Arnold Jacobs. In the summer of 1953 I toured with the Sauter-Finegan Orchestra. I recall the many times Arnold Jacobs came to hear the orchestra at the Blue Note (a Chicago jazz club) and how enthusiastic he was about the role of the tuba. Throughout the 50s, while touring with the U.S. Army Field Band, New York Brass Quintet, New York City Ballet, or appearing at the annual Chicago Mid-

West Band & Orchestra Clinic, we had many pleasant visits over lunch or dinner.

In the summer of 1963 I was invited by Dr. Robert Hawkins to join the Gunnison Music Camp faculty and perform in the Directors Band. This was the most enjoyable and memorable summer of my life. William Bell and Arnold Jacobs were also on the faculty. Performing in the tuba section with these two legendary artists was an experience I shall never forget. The Directors Band did a lot of recording that summer, including one which featured the tuba section performing (in unison) Paganini's "Perpetual Motion." Aggie Bell, Gizzy Jacobs, and my wife Carol also thoroughly enjoyed the summer activities; when we weren't teaching, rehearsing, or performing, we were partying. Little wonder that the summer of 1963 was an absolute highlight of my life in music.

It is always pleasant and enlightening to discuss the art of making music with Arnold Jacobs. No one of my acquaintance is more knowledgeable about the art of brass playing, and no one is more articulate than Arnold Jacobs. For over 45 years Arnold Jacobs has been the major influence on tubists who aspire to a career in one of the world's great orchestras. Through the many recordings made by the Chicago Symphony Orchestra during his tenure as solo tubist, his artistry is well documented for future generations to enjoy and aspire to emulate. Through his countless successful and devoted students his teaching techniques and philosophy of life will ever be perpetuated. The legacy of Arnold Jacobs features enormous contributions to brass performance and musical artistry; his students have included vocalists and woodwind players, as well as students of every brass instrument. Every musician who has enjoyed contact with Arnold Jacobs is better for it and eager to reflect Jacobs' influence on their teaching and performance.

Arnold Jacobs is one of a select few artists whose performance artistry has been equaled by his ability to teach and communicate his knowledge and experience. He has proven to be one of the great master teachers of all time. He seems consumed with an insatiable desire to teach others; to mold, shape, inspire and inevitably coerce the maximum potential from every student who seeks his counsel and guidance. As do many of my professor colleagues, I urge all of my students to secure as many lessons as they can manage from him, as many as his schedule will permit. I personally call and arrange for those lessons whenever possible. In addition, I will continue to support invitations for Arnold Jacobs to be a featured panelist at every brass symposium.

My association with Arnold Jacobs has had a profound effect on my life in music. In an art and profession composed of talented performers and dedicated teachers, Arnold Jacobs is very, very special indeed.

Arnold Jacobs, taken by Abe Torchinsky in 1941

George T. Rhodes
Trombone, Formerly Indianapolis Symphony

It is not an exaggeration to say that I owe the last 10 or 11 years of my playing career to Arnold Jacobs. He helped me reverse a certain deterioration in my playing that I was experiencing, and also helped me to continue improving my playing during the remaining years of my career. I compare him to a top-notch medical specialist who is not only an unfailing diagnostician, but who is also able to prescribe the correct cure and rehabilitation of the patient.

After more than 20 successful years as first trombonist with the Indianapolis Symphony, I began to experience some difficulty in making soft attacks in the upper register, an ability in which I had always taken some pride. Other problems developed gradually, one minor frustration here, another there, accumulating over several years to a point where my self-confidence was impaired. When the opportunity to play second trombone presented itself, I was more than happy to step down. Though my pride suffered a bit, I reasoned that I would be under less pressure and would be able to cope more successfully with my problems. I was just over 50 at the time, had always loved making music, and intended to continue doing so, but I realized the need to seek help. I finally decided to give Arnold Jacobs a call, a decision I have never regretted.

I guess all of Jake's former students have fond recollections of the old house on South Normal in Chicago. I drove up from Indianapolis, finally located the house, and was ushered into the living room by Mrs. Jacobs, where I was made to feel at home. I sat on the sofa chatting and playing with the dog while tuba sounds vibrated up through the floor. Finally, it was my turn to follow the labyrinthine path to the basement studio where there was just enough space for Mr. Jacobs and myself, two chairs, and a music stand amidst a conglomeration of clinical devices for measuring lung capacity, tubas of assorted shapes and sizes, electronic equipment, and so on. I hadn't played more than a few notes of warm-up before he had discerned my problems and was ready to begin the process of solving them. I can't remember all the details of that first lesson, but I know that we worked on the mouthpiece separately from the instrument as a tool for producing a full tone through free use of the air and unrestricted lip vibration. I had never believed in mouthpiece practice except as a means of keeping in shape during vacations, but I soon learned that I could transfer the feel and sound achieved on the mouthpiece to the trombone, an important step in the regeneration process.

Jake explained that normal reduction of lung capacity and elasticity commences somewhere around the age of 40. Some players compensate for this by falling into the habit of holding the lower gut tight (isometric action of the breathing apparatus), which causes poor tone and fatigue or lack of endurance, and holding back air with the tongue, which causes poor entrances. This is perhaps an over-simplification of a process that is at first imperceptible and develops insidiously while one is unaware of serious problems. By the time the problems are recognized the bad habits are deeply ingrained and are causing increasing difficulties. I had never had a large lung capacity, but the fantastic performance of Jacobs with less capacity than mine encouraged me to believe that I could learn to make much more efficient use of my own equipment.

One doesn't change ingrained habits overnight. In fact, Jake advised, "Don't try to change old habits; work on developing new habits." I was able to begin a reversal of the degenerative process, continue to improve, and enjoy my playing until my retirement. For several years I made the trip to Chicago for a lesson whenever I could take the time from a busy playing and teaching schedule. After each lesson I would jot down a few notes to refresh my memory and help me continue the improvements I always made during the lesson. In looking over these notes I find the following: "Think of the end result, the sound;" and "play by wind and song." These quotes might not be significant to the uninitiated, but they are part of his psychology in getting the student to forget the mechanics of playing and to concentrate on making music. By wind he meant the air flowing outside of the mouth, a concept designed to help the student avoid restricting the flow of air with the tongue. "Wind and song, not air pressure and song. Air resistance from the lips only, not from the tongue."

Jake devised many exercises and devices to enable students to accomplish a given task: various breathing exercises, some with the help of a plastic tube or a plastic bag, some with no extraneous devices, but done while looking at a mirror; numerous exercises for various purposes, some performed on trombone, some vocalized, and of course regular mouthpiece practice, especially of orchestral parts prior to practicing them on the trombone. In writing about these details it is not possible for me to convey the importance, the practicality, the ingenuity of these ideas; or, as skeptics might describe some of them, gimmicks. A point to be emphasized is Jacobs' amazing grasp of all the mechanical principles involved, the cause and effect relationships of all parts of the anatomy used in performing, and his great skill in teaching these precepts. A second significant point is his use of psychology in helping the student to understand the prime value of pure musical concepts (sound, song) while working on technical problems. An adjunct to all of this is his obvious love of playing and teaching and the enthusiasm with which he applies himself to each.

Jake always respected my experience and musicianship, and treated me as a colleague in need of help rather than as a student. He understood the difficulty of trying to make changes in my playing while meeting the daily requirements of my job. The psychology paid off here. He advised me to work on technical problems at home, and to just concentrate on making music on the job. "Think positive, not of what can go wrong. Don't fight yourself, enjoy the music."

I learned not to fight myself and to enjoy the music. I was able to add some rewarding years to a satisfying career that, without his skill and understanding, might have come to an early and humiliating close. I am now enjoying retirement after 35 years in the profession. Given the opportunity, I would do it all over again with one exception: I'd study with Jake much earlier, not only for the knowledge to be acquired, but also for the warm friendship to be experienced.

William C. Robinson
French Horn, Baylor University

What is the magic of Arnold Jacobs? Why do his students, not only on tuba and other brass instruments, but on other instruments as well, swear by his teaching? How has he been able to help so many musicians? How is it that he has been able to literally revolutionize the musical abilities and even the lives of so many musicians?

I vividly remember one early morning, while enjoying the bounties of a Mexican breakfast in one of San Antonio's fine restaurants, when a chance conversation changed my musical life. I was visiting with a friend, a fine tuba player, who had studied with Arnold Jacobs. During the course of the conversation, he reiterated a fact which I had heard many times before: "Mr. Jacobs' teaching is just wonderful! He makes you play so well, you just wouldn't believe it." Having heard this same theme many times before from several different musicians, all of whom I respected highly, I was intrigued more than ever. I asked my friend just exactly what it was that Mr. Jacobs did that was so wonderful and awe-inspiring. I wanted to know exactly what methods he used and how he achieved such outstanding results. The only answer I could elicit was, "He makes you sing on the horn. I don't know what he does, but he just makes you play better than you ever have before. He teaches song and wind."

The answer left me unsatisfied and in a state of wonder; then and there I resolved to find out for myself the details of this wonderful way of teaching. I remembered vividly a statement that Dale Clevenger, first hornist of the Chicago Symphony, had made to me. "You should get with Jake; if anything ever happened to my playing, I wouldn't hesitate, I'd run to Jake and he would straighten out my playing."

At this time I was working hard, practicing a great deal each day, being conscientious in my warm-up and etude practice, and getting worse every day! This fact reinforced my decision to go to Mr. Jacobs and learn what I could. I called him by phone from

Waco and arranged some specific times for lessons as soon as I could get to Chicago. When I called him from the hotel in Chicago, I was a little mystified at his reaction. He asked me what I wanted to learn from him; I told him I wanted to learn about correct breathing as it related to playing the horn, whereupon he told me, "Unless you have a medical background, you can't understand it." I responded, "I don't care about knowing all the physical details; I just want to do it and be able to teach my students to do it and thereby improve their playing." He told me that he would help me and to come to his studio in the Fine Arts Building on Michigan Avenue at a specified time.

I will never forget the first ten minutes of that first lesson. First, he asked me to play for him. My performance of the last movement of the Mozart Second Concerto was really not one that an audience would buy tickets to hear. When I finished with my struggles, he said, "I see some talent there, but you have some problems."

He immediately recognized the fact that I had fallen into the trap of concentrating on the action of the embouchure, body muscles, and other technical actions connected with playing a wind instrument. Without warning, he tossed me a pencil, and without thinking, I caught it in mid-air. This simple act drove home to me a point that is probably one of the most important things I have ever learned in horn playing. Mr. Jacobs told me that one cannot control the action of the embouchure by thinking about it and by trying to control the muscles. He said, "You didn't have to think which muscles in your arm and in your fingers you needed to use to catch the pencil. You instinctively wanted to catch the pencil and your brain, which is the greatest computer ever created, relayed the message to each muscle involved. You cannot control the muscles by trying to control the muscles. If you want to play a particular tone, put that tone in your mind and in your ear — the exact pitch, the quality you want, the desired volume — then play the tone and the brain will tell the body what to do. This will happen, provided you open the mouth, take a breath, and blow an air column. Sing the pitch in your mind and in your ear, use the air and you are using two principles of playing that are fundamental to artistic playing: song and wind."

Concerning breathing, I must mention a point that made an indelible impression on me and has paved the way for improvement ever since. I had heard that some teachers teach their students not to raise or expand the chest when breathing. They teach the student to breathe down low and use the diaphragm. Mr. Jacobs, while sitting next to me on my right, said, "This is what breath support is all about." Then he simply opened his mouth, let the air rush in, and blew a vibrant air column. When he inhaled, his chest must have expanded toward the front at least six inches, or so it seemed to me. He told me not to think about what happens in the various parts of the body when breathing; just open the mouth, take in the air, then blow an air column. This approach immediately made me feel free of a great many tone-destroying habits into which I had fallen in recent years. Coupled with that, he pointed out the necessity for exaggeration in singing a phrase. Of course I knew this, but I had overlooked the whole concept while playing because I was so concerned with the technical problems and procedures, which in reality were doing nothing but tying me in knots when I tried to play.

My first contact with Mr. Jacobs was during the summer of 1977. I subsequently returned for more lessons during the summers of 1978 and 1979. At every lesson I learned many things; always, at each lesson, I learned some gem of knowledge which triggered many improvements and new practice methods. These ideas have evolved into a way of playing which is not only gratifying to me and to the listener, but they have enabled me to improve my playing consistently, with an ease I would never have thought possible. Most of these triggering thoughts are so simple that it's easy to wonder how they could have been overlooked for so long. I think this is where the problem lies. These important facets of playing are so profound, yet so simple, that they can easily be overlooked.

One of these gems has been so important to me and to my playing and teaching that it bears amplification. At one point in a lesson Mr. Jacobs had me play a tone and then said, "When you get to the middle of the tone your sound is good. Now, just move that sound over to the beginning of the tone." This is a very simple statement, and upon hearing it, it seems basic and obvious. However, if one really puts that principle of playing into use, the results are phenomenal. You cannot do this without using the breath correctly from the beginning of the tone. The breath must move immediately, creating instant tone. This is the basis of constant quality, good articulation, tone control, and the ability to shape a phrase. It also prevents that terrible habit common to so much horn playing — the habit of pushing, ballooning, or twa-twaing the tones. That last descriptive word reminds me of Dale Clevenger and his very definite description of that kind of tone. I should also mention that during the years 1979 to the present I never miss an opportunity to study with him. The fact that Mr. Jacobs and Mr. Clevenger teach the same approach to playing and have done so much to help many students achieve a high degree of artistry is a blessing to us all.

During my first lesson with Mr. Jacobs he asked me if I warmed up carefully before playing. "Oh yes," I replied, "I am very conscientious about warming up." (As a matter of fact, I felt that I could not play until I had done about 45 minutes of warm-up.) Whereupon he said, "Don't warm up, just pick up the horn and play."

When he told me not to warm up, I was skeptical, and in the back of my mind, I thought it wouldn't work. However, after working with him and having a taste of what could really be done with my playing, I was so excited that I could hardly wait to get home and put all the things I learned into practice. Instead of looking forward to a vacation from the horn, as I had been doing, I could hardly wait to get to work.

I realized that Mr. Jacobs did not mean that the warm-up had no value, or that scale practice and etude practice should be forgotten. What he did was free me psychologically from ideas that were handcuffing my playing. He wanted me to think of the music, involve myself in the music, sing on the wind, and pick up the horn and make music.

When I arrived home I was determined to try this idea, still wondering in the back of my mind if it would really work. At seven o'clock the next morning I took the horn and deliberately did not play one note prior to playing the Mendelssohn "Nocturne." To my amazement and gratification, I played it all the way through, better than I had ever played it before. I had always been careful never to play this piece without a thorough warm-up, and even then I had been somewhat apprehensive while playing it. This illustrates the tremendous psychological barriers that often impede our progress. Mr. Jacobs proved to me in a few minutes that most of these hindrances can be removed if we focus our attention on important matters: the music and singing the phrase on the wind.

Can I explain the magic of Arnold Jacobs? I only know that he completely revolutionized my playing; my students now play far better than before, but more important, they enjoy making music much more and our complete attention is on the musical phrase.

When we do a few things right (take in the air and sing the phrase), the problems of embouchure function, bodily action, and other technical matters, which used to occupy so much attention, now seem to have a way of taking care of themselves.

While attending the Horn Workshop in Avignon, France a few years ago I visited the instrument exhibits during the lunch hour, when the area was relatively quiet. While trying out one of the horns, I played the theme from the Ravel "Pavane." I just sang the melody as Mr. Jacobs had taught me to do, without warming up. I wasn't aware that others were present, but at the end of the passage I was astonished to hear spontaneous applause from the three persons in the room, Steve Lewis, Robert Paxman, and Richard Merewether. Steve said to me, "What a beautiful sound; it makes goose bumps on my arm. How do you play such a beautiful sound?" (He had heard some of my former playing!) My response was, "I just did what Mr. Jacobs taught me to do: I moved the sound from the middle of the tone to the beginning and sang on the wind."

When I first went to Mr. Jacobs I was 57 years old, much past the age when one's playing normally improves. My thought is this concerning his magic: What he has done for me is truly beyond expectations. I will forever be grateful to him and join the legions of others whose lives have forever been enhanced by contact with this great man.

Michael Sanders
Tuba, San Antonio Symphony

I first heard about Arnold Jacobs when I was an aspiring high school tuba player growing up in the suburbs of Washington, D.C. As I look back on this time it was a particularly fruitful one for me because the four major Service bands were headquartered in Washington. For a brief period in the late 1960s the U.S. Army Band tuba section included, among others, Dan Perantoni, Jim Self, and Chester Schmitz. I was lucky to study with several people who had graduated from major music schools and had then gone to Washington to do military service. When it came to the tuba players they most admired, Arnold Jacobs was always mentioned. Being young and impressionable, a good deal of this information stuck with me, but much of it went out the other ear.

One day when I had enough money to spare, I bought the Fritz Reiner recording of *Pictures at an Exhibition*, mostly because I liked the cover art, and some notes on the back of it mentioned a tuba. I was quite taken with the sound of the brass, especially in the "Catacombs" and "The Great Gate," and I told my teacher that I thought the brass sounded like the Marine Band. Ah, youth! He then made the connection for me between Arnold Jacobs, the tuba player and the subject of conversation, and Arnold Jacobs' sound in the great Chicago Symphony brass section.

Over the next few years in my own compulsive, provincial way, I proceeded to buy as many C.S.O. recordings as I could find and afford. Why? Because you can hear the tuba, of course.

Time went by, and my tuba playing began to get better. I went through all the contests and festivals that high school players go through and ended up at Eastman. It was in my junior year during Thanksgiving vacation that I met Arnold Jacobs for the first time. With the encouragement of Donald Knaub, my teacher at Eastman, Doug Purvis (another tuba player at E.S.M., now in the Canadian Ballet orchestra) and I made the trip to Chicago, to that well-known address on South Normal Avenue.

So it was all true — the staircase down to the basement full of tubas and charts and equipment, the string bass in the corner, and the man himself with the resonant voice and the friendly, firm handshake. Naturally, I was completely bowled over, particularly by the immense knowledge the man had; it was too much to absorb all at once. I remember clearly nearing the end of my time limit at that first lesson. Mr. Jacobs asked if I had any questions. "Is there anything else?" he asked, looking at me with a smile. "I would like to hear you play," I replied. He winked, slapped me on the thigh, and said, "Of course, they all do."

When he played, I took in as much as I could, I listened and watched as he gave me his rendition of some little tune. We all know that sound and that espressivo quality that is Arnold Jacobs, but I also remember the tremendous happiness and pride that was so obvious in this great performer.

More time went by, and I continued to visit Chicago several times a year. I joined the San Antonio Symphony in September 1973, and that meant I could afford to go to Chicago several times a year and spend two or three weeks of my summer vacation there. I did this, and the more time I spent in his studio, the clearer his message became. In my first two or three lessons there had been so much information to assimilate that at times I over analyzed, but the continuity made it much clearer. All this information about breathing and the other physical aspects of playing was merely the means to an end, the art form.

This is really the greatest message we receive from Arnold Jacobs. He helps us with all our problems, but he continually urges us to perform. He wants us to tell a story with the music we play. We don't have to be playing the last movement of the Hindemith on a beautiful new tuba. We can be playing "Row, Row, Row Your Boat" on a mouthpiece, and it is all the same to him. And it needs to be for us.

There are many times I have called Arnold Jacobs for advice about an instrument, or for support before or after an audition. The last time I actually saw him was in 1979 during the Mid-west Band and Orchestra Convention. I was involved in a convention clinic with Don Little, Everett Gilmore, and Steve Bryant. I made the effort to go to a concert by the C.S.O. even though it was a sell-out, and I was able to get in. The performance was great, and it was wonderful to hear that brass section again. I met Jake at the door after the concert and talked him into coming back to the hotel for a couple of beers. We walked into the bar and saw Ev Gilmore and Jim Self. Naturally we all gathered at one table and had about an hour of great conversation. When the time came for Jake to leave he made the attempt to pay for the entire get-together, but the three of us all chimed in together and insisted it was on us. It was truly our pleasure.

William Scarlett
Trumpet, Chicago Symphony

My association with Arnold Jacobs began when I was a student in Chicago and listened to him at Orchestra Hall, playing the tuba with the fluency of an old-time cornet player. Having grown up with a cornet in my hand, my reaction was one of disbelief. How could anyone skip around on a tuba so easily? This made an important impression on me that would be used later in my development.

During my college years I learned more about this wonderful tuba player. I also learned that his reputation as a teacher was as high as his reputation as a player, and that woodwind and voice students were as eager as brass students to learn from him. After finishing college I felt I needed more ideas, ideas that corresponded to what I had heard about the expertise of Arnold Jacobs. Having met him many times while playing as an extra with the Chicago Symphony during my college years, I was eager to begin working with him as a student.

The first lesson was an unforgettable experience. Surely I was impressed with all of this medical equipment and with all of those long words that I had not heard before; but the part of the lesson that Jacobs says he remembers was when he checked my vital capacity (lung capacity). The spirometer he was using had a bell suspended in a liquid; when I blew on a hose that emptied under the bell, the bell lifted until it went right out of the liquid, well past the scale on the side for checking the vital capacity. Jacobs was flustered and couldn't figure how I could ruin his set-up so easily. He gave me a careful lesson again on what to do; "keep your mouth tight around the tube," as well as other warnings. Again we went through the routine and again the bell lifted out of the liquid. At this point he just sat back, chuckled and said, "You're a freak! With lungs the size of yours you should have a body six feet six."

Weekly lessons continued during that first summer of my enjoyable study. After each lesson I went straight home and wrote down every word he had said. These lessons were relived many times, especially during my two years of service for Uncle Sam in Germany. Upon returning from Germany, my lessons continued in that Normal Avenue basement.

Everyone has key ingredients in his development. In my own case there is no doubt at all that without the help of Arnold Jacobs, I would not be an orchestral player today. His ideas of inspired playing combined with efficient physical delivery of air to the embouchure have helped so many of us from all over the music world.

Today, even after playing in the same orchestra with Jake for 20 years, my respect for his playing and teaching continues to grow. He never stops searching for a better idea. There is ample evidence of his value to the profession from his recordings, from the number of his graduates, and by the steady stream of students and professionals who come to Chicago from distant cities to get help.

Much more can be said about the professional side of Arnold, but when I think of him, I think of a marvelous, warm human being. He always wears a smile and has a friendly hello; there's always time for a chat; there's always a willingness to talk shop. This never changes, even when everyone knows that personal thoughts are foremost in his mind.

My hat is off to Jake in this tribute. I thank him for his knowledge, I thank him for his encouragement, but above all, I thank him for his warm friendship.

Left to right, Ron Bishop, Arnold Jacobs, and Michael Lind, on Michigan Avenue, Chicago, July 1982

74

Paul T. Severson
Trombonist, Composer/arranger

My first awareness of Arnold Jacobs came while performing in Ralph Marterie's orchestra with a fine bass trombonist by the name of Gene Isaeff. I admired Gene's tone quality and the ease with which he played. It wasn't many days before we began to compare our formative backgrounds and the teachers with whom we had studied. Gene was most complimentary about Arnold Jacobs, so on my next trip back to Chicago, I contacted Arnold and scheduled a lesson time. Little did I know that this was to be the start of an association that would last more than ten years.

My first lesson was possibly one of the most important and memorable lessons in my musical life. After a few moments of getting acquainted he asked me to warm up. He picked out a fairly simple Rochut etude and asked me to play it. I proceeded to play as best I could and after several phrases he stopped me and said, "I can tell that you are a well-trained musician and probably play other instruments as well." (I played piano quite well). "The secret in playing," he continued, "is to pre-hear the complete tromboneness of the trombone in your musical imagination. I have a feeling that while you sensed much of the musical quality and value of the etude, you did not approach it as a trombone artist. Artistry can only be channeled through creative imagination and you must concentrate on the exact results you want before you perform."

I had been vaguely aware of positive thinking and motivational research prior to this lesson, but somehow Arnold made it all make sense. He then added another observation. "As you played this etude you increased your trombone sound awareness, but every time you stopped and started again you were in jeopardy. Missed notes, poorly articulated attacks, and mediocre tone quality result from fuzzy mental imagination."

That was a lot of advice for one lesson, or even a lifetime of study, and I got it in the first ten minutes of my first lesson. Up to this time I believed that you would automatically get better if you just put in more practice time. Arnold's concept challenged mine and also excited me with new hope of musical advancement. I decided then to pursue a long association as a student of Arnold's, and happily, he accepted me as a student.

In a variety of ways he helped me to survive the rigors of the Stan Kenton Orchestra, the Hal McIntyre Orchestra, the Chicago Civic Orchestra, the Chicago Theater, and eight years as a solo trombonist at C.B.S. in Chicago.

One of the most indelible memories of every lesson was his ability to challenge me with various exercises and to get me to play some passage or figure that had been impossible for me to execute. It was great to leave a lesson knowing that even the most difficult trombone literature could be possible for me to perform. Arnold had the ability to musically psych me into a frame of mind so that I played successfully more often.

In almost every lesson we spent time on the simple principle of producing good, consistent tone quality and the necessity of carrying that quality to all registers, to every note, long or short, loud or soft. Arnold listened intently to every note I played and often watched me from different vantage points to observe the physical processes as well as musical results. I often felt naked. It seemed that nothing in my playing escaped his attention. I always felt he was sincerely interested in me and my playing, and his constant care and attention was a powerful motivating force for me as a student. He was never perfunctory in his attitude or manner towards me and my efforts. I felt that I owned him for 60 minutes an hour, or possibly he owned me. I never came to him with a difficult playing problem that he couldn't understand and show me how to solve. This resource for problem solving gave me a marvelous feeling of security in the very insecure business of instrumental performance.

The other mark of Arnold's teaching genius was the sense of his presence when I practiced alone. Long after I left the Chicago area I could feel him beside me; this impression is still with me today. When I sit down to practice I can still hear his words, phrases, gentle rejoinders when I am not doing my best, and his spontaneous excitement when new successes arrive. "Yes, yes, yes." I can still hear him.

The second phase of our relationship occurred in a very unique way. After leaving C.B.S., I went into free-lance arranging and composing for T.V. and radio commercials, industrial films, and records. When contracting musicians for recording sessions I had Arnold play tuba on many dates over a 12-year period. In this way we were able to continue our warm personal and musical association.

In 1973 I decided to semi-retire and leave the Chicago area. I had been so busy writing during these 12 years that I finally stopped practicing and performing on trombone. However, before I left Chicago I knew I wanted to play trombone again, so I contacted Arnold once more for his special advice and council. Not surprisingly, he reiterated his advice from my first lesson. He stressed the fact that even though I had been a trombonist for many years and an avid trombone fan during my writing years, I would almost certainly have lost much of the inner mental creation of tromboneness. Once I could stir that creative picture to the forefront again, the rest of the process of strengthening the proper lip and facial muscles would be relatively easy if I had enough patience. And always, always, he said to aim for consistent quality. Arnold was right on all counts. In a moderately short period of time I was playing and performing again with much of the ease and joy of my former years.

I found Arnold Jacobs to be a consummate artist in his own milieu. As a teacher he was always vitally interested in me both musically and personally. He understood human frailties, weaknesses, and lack of motivation, and he knew that a student would only work to the degree that it was important to the student's real priorities. I also found Arnold to be a sensitive performer in the many sessions I arranged, composed, or conducted; I always knew his results would be consistently excellent.

All of this was such a part of my life at the time that I didn't realize the complete value of my association with him until I reflected on it later in life. In his relationship with me, Arnold was kind, sincere, honest (always saving my dignity), interested, involved, and concerned. In all the ways we related to each other, nothing was more important than our friendship; and until I wrote this I didn't realize how much I miss him.

The legacy of his influence will never be assessed exactly, but wherever brass players assemble and talk about instructors, I mention my years with Arnold Jacobs and the inevitable response is, "Do you know how lucky you are?" "You studied 10 years with a master." "What I wouldn't give to study with him!"

Thank you, Arnold. I'll pass on what you taught me in the best way I can, so your legacy will continue as long as there are brass instruments and music making.

Susan Slaughter
Trumpet, St. Louis Symphony

My first lesson with Arnold Jacobs was July 5, 1971; I was 26 years of age. Our principal horn in St. Louis was Roland Pandolfi, who had studied with Arnold Jacobs when Roland was principal in Milwaukee. My problem? I had become tight, using far more physical energy than necessary to produce the sound, which at times shattered on me.

The first thing Jacobs did was measure my air capacity by inserting a tube into my mouth. I inhaled as much as possible, sealed my lips around the tube, and exhaled the air as fast as possible. My capacity was about 3.5 liters of air. "Very good considering your height," Jacobs said. For me, the best part of that exercise was when I inserted the tube into my mouth. My tongue went down, which allowed me to take a free, full breath. We worked on a number of exercises without the trumpet. For example:

- Place your thumb in your mouth to form the opening to bring in the air; think of sucking on a straw.
- Take air in; breathe in 1/3, 2/3, then full capacity, hold, let the air out. Practice variations on this exercise, then take in 2/3, 1/3, then let out 2/3, out 1/3.
- Do not try to correct what is wrong by fixing the lips a certain way; work and listen for the sound, not for feeling.
- Sit erect for one year, very erect.
- Work on using vowels to keep the tongue down, use the word "toe."
- Take full breaths using the "bag" (the bag was a cellophane bag that held five liters of air; it had a tube coming out of it so that you could inhale and exhale in and out of the bag without hyperventilating).
- Fill up capacity of the mouthpiece with air, listening for sound.
- When exhaling do not try to force air out, but don't hold air back, let it out naturally.

Jacobs measured lung capacity with an instrument that looked like two blood pressure gauges with one tube connected to one gauge and a second tube connected to the other gauge. Both tubes were connected to each other in the center with a single tube serving as the main access to the two gauges.

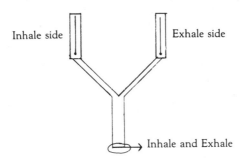

Each gauge had a ball inside. When inhaling, the idea was to use the air to pull the ball up to a certain number (mine was 30) and maintain the ball at that position until it started to fluctuate. When exhaling the object was to watch the ball in the other gauge and make it stay at 30 until it started to fluctuate, then inhale again, repeating the cycle.

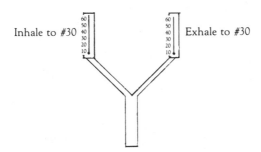

The key to this exercise is to watch for the fluctuation of the ball. When this occurs on the inhale side it means you cannot take in any more air and it is time to start exhaling. When the ball fluctuates on the exhale side it means you have gotten out all of the air possible (without tension), and you should start to inhale again and keep repeating this cycle. Another benefit to this exercise is that it illustrates how we tend to overblow on the exhale side, using far too much energy to exhale.

Jacobs charts breathing capacity in the following way:

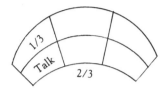

We should play with the upper 2/3 of our air capacity and never enter into the last 1/3: this is the air we use to talk. When we reach the last 1/3 of air in exhalation, the ball in the gauge will begin to fluctuate and it's time to take a breath.

My first assignment involved a great deal of work away from the instrument, although some of the material Jacobs had me work on did include the instrument.

Charlier — Etude No.2

Schlossberg — #26, #27, #36 — 2-note phrases.

#52 ♩♩♩ | ♩♩♩ all slurred

#145 — not too slow — in 3 — no crescendo.

• For 1/2 hour a day, play on the mouthpiece alone, use lots of vibrato, play songs, check pitches with a strobe tuner.

• Concentrate on the sound at mf-f level.

• When practicing scales, work on the starting tone; make the starting tone the same as the final tone, full.

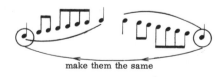

make them the same

- Work with a mouthpiece only, (depressing valves at same time) — first tones must be full.

- Attack with a full sound, not a round attack.
- When playing long phrases, do not hold the air back; break the phrase up, and take a full breath at each breath spot. Do not try to retain air, but let the body act like a bellows, always free to expand to its fullest, always concentrating on the sound regardless of the volume.

Jacobs told me, "When playing make statements, don't ask questions. Recondition the thought process. Produce the sound you want to hear; do not think about mechanics. Get and maintain that sound throughout the whole passage. Equalize the mouthpiece pressure when playing and buzzing; use more pressure on all four points of contact."

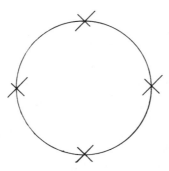

When buzzing the mouthpiece, he told me to be musical, play melodies, use more pressure when buzzing, and don't feel, play! Skip a warm-up, play melodies at mf and mp levels. Don't try to feel a note before you play it. Have a concept of sound, breathe, then play with that concept of sound. Attacks will improve and will be more secure. Let your concept of sound tell the muscles and breath what to do naturally, don't try to order the lips or tongue. Use vowels. Sound, not feeling.

In the upper register play on the lower side of the pitch, let the notes be flat when practicing. Work with the mouthpiece only and watch a strobe tuner, learn to buzz pitches on pitch or even below pitch. Play fourth space E open and with 3rd valve. Learn to know where the note is without strain. Work on scales into the trouble area.

Other important advice I received from Jacobs included:

• Breathe in thirds of air capacity. Suck the air in; do not cause rib cage to move unless the movement is done naturally. Learn to drop diaphragm down more — around the belt level.

• Play songs in the upper octave using lots of vibrato.

• Practice the high register in the mf level. Learn to know what the note feels like by the second or third beat, then relax, re-attack the note with right sound. Do not try to feel the note; missed notes do not matter during this kind of practice.

• Play a lot on the piccolo trumpet; play simple melodies in the middle to high register using lots of vibrato and resting frequently.

• Work on these exercises:

• Play the same note, and by the second beat get the feel and follow-through established, then learn to initiate this on the first beat with the attack. Prepare the sound, not the attack.

• Remember to think about sound, not attack. Sound, not muscle activity. Sound, not tension. Sound.

• When reaching the end of the air supply, learn to move the diaphragm up faster and tighter to move that last third of air more rapidly, especially when a high note comes at the end of a phrase.

• Equalize pressure on the mouthpiece, especially when playing up higher. When attacking in the upper register make sure contact is made with the lower lip before initial attack is attempted.

• Sit erect, not tense, but get the rib cage out of way of the diaphragm.

Ross Tolbert
Tuba, Minnesota Orchestra

As a professional musician and teacher for many years, I have come across all types of musicians and teachers. Several names come to mind when I think of great musicians, and a comparable number appear in the category of great teachers, but very few fit into both categories. Not only does Arnold Jacobs fit into both categories, he ranks at the very top of each.

My first impression of Arnold came in my late teens. Having already gained an appreciation for the tuba and the symphony orchestra, I listened intently to any recordings I could find. One day I obtained a recording of the Prokofiev *Lieutenant Kijé* performed by Fritz Reiner and the Chicago Symphony Orchestra. I could not believe the magnificent tuba sounds. "Who is this sound machine?" I asked myself. Intent on finding the answer, I didn't have to ask many of my musician friends before the name was revealed — Arnold Jacobs. From that point on, I sought out every Chicago Symphony recording I could find. Without question, my finest listening hours in those days were spent with Reiner, the Chicago Symphony, and with my new-found mentor, Arnold Jacobs.

Not too long after my discovery, I was fortunate enough to become the tuba player with the New Orleans Symphony. Another stroke of good fortune occurred there when I found a marvelous trombone section consisting of Ned Meredith, Glenn Dodson, and Dee Stewart. Dee was a Jacobs student, and I consistently bent his ear to try to learn whatever I could about his teacher. Dee was more than encouraging and saw to it that I got to Chicago to meet Arnold. At one point Dee even shared his Chicago trailer home to make it easier for me to study.

My first lesson was not a very pleasant experience, but an inevitable awakening. Having a symphony job had given me a false sense of security. I thought I could walk in, play a few notes, and walk out with some rave comments to feed my ego. I was wrong. Actually, when I left from this lesson I wondered if I would ever again have an ego. Arnold wasn't really unkind, just truthful. Everything seemed like a disaster. I used barely half my breathing capacity, air pressure measured out of proportion, I had no relaxation, and no ideal mental image of sound. What would I do? The thought of leaving town surfaced in my mind, but only briefly. Despite this revelation of all my problems, Arnold somehow managed to convey that it was possible for me to overcome them. I knew I would be back. By the end of this first set of four lessons, I felt much better. Arnold spoke positively about my future, and couldn't have been more encouraging.

In the years following I made several more trips to Chicago, the last when I was in my early 30s. I always left with fresh determination. Arnold could play two or three notes and suddenly I would feel an overwhelming desire to play, to express. It was the same feeling I had when I first heard the *Kijé* recording years before. Incredibly few musicians have the wonderful ability to move an audience. Arnold Jacobs is one of those wonderful and incredible few.

Abe Torchinsky
Instructor of Tuba, Michigan University

I first met Arnold Jacobs around 1934. I was 14 at the time and Arnold was 19. He was a student of Philip Donatelli at the Curtis Institute of Music in Philadelphia and I had been taking lessons from a student of his, Bob McCandless. My brother, who was an excellent musician, thought I had talent and realizing that Arnold was the best teacher available in the Philadelphia area, he spoke to Arnold, who accepted me as a student. His fee at that time was $1.00 for an indefinite time. I traveled to Arnold's home in north Philadelphia by a variety of trolley cars, carrying my tuba and whatever music I needed.

After Arnold went to the Indianapolis Symphony, I studied with him whenever he came back to Philadelphia. I remember an incident when Arnold's son, Dallas, was an infant in his crib. I was taking a lesson sitting next to the crib. Dallas picked up a round empty candy tin and hit me on the head. I'm not sure whether he was displeased with my playing or he was admonishing me to practice. In any case, many years later we still get a big kick out of the incident.

Arnold was instrumental in two important parts of my musical career. He, along with my brother, insisted I play string bass. This turned out to be important, because the bass financed my tuba studying until I was successful as a tubist. I am deeply grateful to him for insisting on that. He also recommended me for my first symphony job, the Southern Symphony under Hans Schwieger in Columbia, South Carolina, 1938-39. The season was 10 weeks and payed $27.50 per week. This may not sound like much to some of the younger players, but this was my first break. This experience helped me to get into Curtis Institute and from there my career went ahead.

As young as Arnold was at the time I studied with him, I learned a tremendous amount. Most of all I learned to enjoy music — all kinds of music. He made me work but enjoy the work. Even then his approach to the psychology of music was very evident. To this day when I teach I try to use much of the approach that I learned from Arnold 50 years ago.

I'm proud to consider him as one of my special friends and even prouder to have been one of his peers during my tenure as an orchestra player.

85

Robert Tucci
Tuba, Bavarian State Opera Orchestra

My first tuba teacher was Harold McDonald, tubist with the Pittsburgh Symphony Orchestra for 25 years. Mac had studied with Jake after World War II. When I had my first lesson with Mac in 1955, I heard a real symphonic tuba sound for the first time in my life. Mac always had the highest respect for Jake and for the brass players in Chicago, and made no secret of the fact that what he was trying to teach me was Jake's concept of playing. So I got to know Arnold even before meeting him in 1958, when he was 43 years old and at the height of his career during the famous Reiner years. His playing still fascinates me today, but to my youthful ears, it was indescribably beautiful, perfect, and alive in every way. His teaching was flabbergasting at first, and it took me years to absorb it and to develop my own playing to a usable and reliable point.

Just as he is now, Jake was full of life and vigor, and was always charming and witty; his life was centered around the tuba, the orchestra, his colleagues, and his students. The orchestra concerts were always amazing. No one liked Reiner, but everyone respected him. At the time the orchestra was doing one particularly difficult and challenging work after another on a week-to-week basis. The concerts were always meticulous; Jake and the brass section seemed to achieve new heights at every moment. It was a unique group of musicians, and even though the strain of playing under Reiner must have been great, everyone was happy and joking all the time. Jake possesses a positive and optimistic nature anyhow; perhaps it rubbed off on others. That is not to say that Adolf Herseth and Ed Kleinhammer were less optimistic; I cannot remember seeing either of them do anything but be happy and smile, either.

During my two years in Chicago (1958-60) I had two opportunities to play with Jake in the orchestra. One was a set of concerts with Igor Markevitch with the Berlioz *Symphonie Fantastique* on the program; the other involved some concerts with Reiner doing Strauss' *Also Sprach Zarathustra*. Jake asked me not to sit too close to him for the Berlioz, and as it turned out, it was good advice; when he let loose in the Dies Irae, all I could do was hang on

86

for dear life. I had heard some big brass sounds from a distance, but sitting that close to Jake and that brass section, with Kleinhammer to one side and Philip Farkas in front, was like standing close to the tracks when an express train goes through. I can still hear those magnificent and glorious sounds today; it went through to the marrow of my bones.

The concerts with Reiner were the most interesting. I never seemed to be able to catch on to his style of conducting, so Jake would give me the cues. Again, this was an experience of a lifetime, to be able to sit in the midst of the greatest orchestra and hear all those glorious sounds close up for the first time. I remember hearing many conversations during the rehearsals about the little man up front. The last of the concerts I played was in the Pabst Theatre in Milwaukee. I went out with Jake, Bob Lambert, and Herseth for dinner before the performance. They ordered big steak dinners, so I did too, but they also ordered double martinis, which I didn't. If my memory serves me correctly, they put down seven each and still played like gods; that was a shock I have not gotten over yet.

My experience with the Chicago Symphony did not go beyond that. Jake probably felt I was getting into his hair too much; I don't think he ever had a more enthusiastic student. One day I was at his house for a lesson when Art Hicks, another student of his from Louisville, called to tell Jake he was going to take a position with the Israel Philharmonic; Hicks needed someone to replace him in Louisville. I had the good fortune to be the lucky boy in Jake's studio at the time. He made some calls to Robert Whitney, conductor of the Louisville Orchestra and an old friend of his from Chicago, and somehow after a short and most informal audition, I had my first job. Louisville also needed someone to replace Hicks as property manager so I had some real responsibility!

My first concert with the Louisville Orchestra was a pre-season engagement, at a health resort in French Lick, Indiana with Arthur Fiedler. Between the dress rehearsal and that first concert a trumpet player and I ended up having one of those "seven double martini" dinners. As it turned out, I couldn't play like Jake, and I couldn't drink like him either. All I remember was Fiedler flailing his arms at me, trying to get me back into tempo somewhere in the heat of the battle in the *Meistersinger* Prelude. When the concert was over, he said, "Young man, the only person out there tonight drunker than me was you." He was very nice about it, but needless to say, I don't drink anymore before concerts.

The two years in Louisville were busy but wonderful. I got to know many fine people, a lovely city and state, and I started learning how to be an orchestral musician. Several of us would go to Chicago whenever possible for lessons. There was no interstate highway between Indianapolis and Chicago then and some of those trips in the middle of midwest winters were pretty wild. One horn player friend heard me talking so much about how great Jake was, he decided to join us for a trip and have a lesson. He said: "If he is as great as you say, I'll eat my hat." We had our trip up there, and it was a snowstorm battle all the way. We heard a great C.S.O. concert one day and had our lessons the next. As we started back to Louisville, my horn player friend was very quiet. We all looked at him and he said, "Pass the salt."

Jake taught me a concept of the tuba, of brass playing, and of musicianship that is of the highest standard. In every lesson he tried to get me fired up, to make music, to make a vibrant and resonant sound come out of the instrument. Every minute with him was full of information about music, the techniques of playing, equipment, and having that same constructive and open-minded approach he has. It all seemed complicated and unattainable at the time, but now I see it was the most logical approach to take.

Over the years I realized that Jake was not only generous with his knowledge and inspiration, but equally generous with himself. He always had the orchestra schedule and his own practice to look after, his home and family, but he seemed to know each of his dozens of students as though they were his children. I guess any man of genius has great memory capabilities. Jake's mental file on each student was always up-to-date, whether a week, month, or year had elapsed between lessons. It seems from my own experience that there is no more demanding or tiring work than teaching privately; Jake's love of and dedication to this activity amazes me even more when I consider he had 32 private students weekly, and every lesson was full application on his part from the first minute to the last.

There has been hardly a day in my life that I haven't had Arnold in my mind: when I pick up the mouthpiece, I see him there with his embouchure rim in hand, making those beautiful sounds; when I pick up the instrument, I see him there wrapped around his beloved York tuba. I love him like a father — that smile, the deep voice, and the heart that is so full of life itself.

Charles Vernon
Bass Trombone, Chicago Symphony Orchestra

I will never forget my first trip to Chicago — 625 miles in a V.W. bug with Harry Maddox. We checked into a hotel and warmed up in preparation for our first lesson with the master; I remember the mushy way I sounded in the hotel room and how I expected to be transformed.

We found our way to the Jacobs house on South Normal, which was located in a rather frightening neighborhood. I'll never forget going up to his door and knocking; the door opened and this stocky, jolly-looking man spoke in the most resonant voice I had ever heard: "Hello, boys, come on in." We could barely get from the door to the living room because of the stacks of newspapers and books piled up the sides of the walls. It was incredible; it made me feel right at home. Jake took Harry downstairs and I went into the living room where his wife and mother-in-law were watching T.V. We spoke a little; Mrs. Jacobs asked about me and she advised me never to marry an artist.

Finally, it was my turn and after risking life and limb getting down into the cellar, I found my way to a little corner surrounded by medical machines, tubes, gauges, and dials. I took my seat to the left of the master. He asked me to warm up for him, and as I proceeded to take a big glass water bottle out of my gig bag I suddenly dropped it right between us on the floor; glass and water went everywhere. I tried to apologize, but the whole incident didn't phase him; he was waiting for me to blow the trombone. After I played a few notes for him, he knew exactly what I was and should be doing. Then I played about four measures of Rochut No. 2, which was all I seemed to ever get out before he stopped me. Jacobs proceeded to give me the most profound, yet simple concepts. When he told me to imagine the most beautiful trombone sound in the world and what it would actually sound like in my head, my first thought was, "How corny, I want to know how to play great," but he never told me. He was very insistent about this concept, and the next time I played the opening slur, it was completely different and, of course, sounded much better. Jacobs' concept of song and wind is so simple that most people won't buy it because it's not complicated enough. Sometimes it was difficult to comprehend him because of his scientific way of speech.

Sometime during that first lesson, after he had torn me down to the basics, he added, "You have an edge over many players musically," and slapped me on the arm. It was a perfectly timed comment, and gave me exactly the motivation that I needed at that time. I was in such awe, floating on an inspirational cloud, that when I got to the door, he reminded me that I owed him $20; how embarrassing.

All my lessons were equally inspiring and uplifting. Song and wind and the psychology of putting forth a positive and aggressive approach to playing were the things he stressed the most. Sometimes, when I would get down or lose sight of the incredible excited and motivated feeling of playing he talked about, I would call and talk to him. Just the resonant sound of his "Hello" was almost enough to bring me back.

In some lessons he was very hard on me and rightfully so. I remember the fourth lesson I had with him; I had been playing with a rock group, "Paul Revere and the Raiders," made some extra money, and bought a Holton bass trombone. About a week later Harry and I went to Chicago for lessons with Jake and Kleinhammer. After playing mostly tenor, I was trying to get into the bass trombone and wasn't ready to have a lesson with Jacobs. He reamed me out and told me that he didn't see or hear any improvement in my playing over the last year and a half.

It was two or three years later when I had my next lesson. During that time I had called him on several occasions for inspiration, but one reason that I took so long to go back for a lesson again was because I didn't want to play badly for him. I have never felt that I played my best for him even in the last couple of lessons. I guess that every student needs approval from his teacher to improve and go onward.

Arnold Jacobs, taken by Robert Tucci

Paul Walton
Tuba, Formerly Minneapolis Orchestra

I met Arnold Jacobs in 1947 when the Chicago Symphony was on tour; he came to my parents' home and gave me a lesson. As a result of this, I went to Chicago on a weekly basis for the next year and a half and eventually moved to Chicago. In 1959 I lived one-half block from Arnold's house on Normal Avenue in south Chicago. Being so close I probably spent more time with Arnold than anyone. He was deeply interested in the breathing mechanism and in lung function as it related to playing wind instruments. What he didn't know about physiology and pulmonary function he learned. Every trip to Orchestra Hall and back on the Illinois Central was a study period. His briefcase was full of the books he needed to understand the medical texts on lung function and respiration as it applied to playing. He was accepted by many people in thoracic medicine as their peer.

Arnold acquired a McKesson vitalator, an instrument used to measure vital capacity. A short time later a tuba player, Dr. Bruce Douglass of the Mayo Clinic, gave him a used spirometer to further his research on breathing.

I remember when the Mayo spirometer arrived. Arnold called me over to help assemble it. We finally got the thing going, only to discover that the machine was missing one small part. After we managed to make the part, Arnold was on his way.

Next came an avalanche of flow meters, special vented mouthpieces, pressure gauges, and other odd-looking inventions. Arnold kept busy taking measurements as they related to playing. Some time later he discovered that an advanced model spirometer was available. This one recorded air flow and lung capacity on a graph. With this new appliance he measured the breath capacity of many professional brass players as well as the saxophone virtuoso, Sigurd Rasher. Arnold was beseiged by woodwind players, horn players, and many trombonists, in addition to his abundant supply of tuba students. Some were professional players, who were in real trouble and concerned about losing their jobs; I know of at least five that were helped, who were restored to being competent plus players.

Some traveled a distance of 500 miles to see him. The reason was results.

Next to music Arnold's great love is people; he enjoys humor even when the joke is on himself. One afternoon I stopped by the Jacobs home to find quite a disaster. Arnold had attempted to repair a sash cord in the dining room window. Somehow, the hammer slipped and he smashed the window pane. Arnold just stood and laughed; we went to a hardware store and got a new pane and replaced the broken cord — peace again in the household. After dinner Arnold put a Schilke adjustable cup mouthpiece in my hand. I had longed for one, but money was short; suddenly I became the most overpaid window repairman in history.

Arnold went on a vacation to Florida one summer for a couple of weeks. He took a mouthpiece, but didn't touch a tuba. I used his studio when I could and for some reason turned on the tape recorder: I heard Arnold getting in shape after having two weeks off. His favorite test of being in top form was a Schlossberg exercise, No. 154. Arnold could crack it off without nicking a note; he started and then in the beginning of the most difficult measure, he hit a clam. He coughed and started over only to get a few notes further, then hit another clinker. Then he stopped and from the tape recorder came a blast of profanity that would do any mule skinner justice. I never told him I eavesdropped, but the next time we played, he cracked off Schlossberg No. 154 — allegro con brio the first time, and it was perfect.

Frank Tritton was a tuba player in Sousa's band in the late 1920s and early 30s; he also did well jobbing in Chicago. When another teacher in Chicago tried to change his embouchure, Frank's playing got worse and worse until he couldn't play at all. He got another job outside of playing and did well, but he dearly missed the tuba. Tritton went to Arnold and they worked together. I was around then and remember thinking that Frank was an impossible case. Yet one summer later Frank could play again. I heard him the following year and he was better still. Frank had the desire to play, and Arnold had the knowledge and patience to help him relearn how to get air going through a tuba to create musical playing. This is a part of the legend of Arnold Jacobs.

Milan Yancich
French Horn, Eastman School of Music

My first association with Arnold Jacobs was as a listener of the Chicago Symphony Orchestra concerts. I was stationed near Chicago at Fort Sheridan during World War II. Whenever possible I attended concerts both at Orchestra Hall in downtown Chicago and at Ravinia Park. It was then that I became acquainted with Arnold Jacobs' great tuba playing. I believe now that if I had begun my studies with him at that time instead of years later, my career as a horn player would have been much more advanced.

When I did begin studying with him, it was during a critical time, and he helped turn around my career as a performer.

In 1948 I became a member of the Chicago Symphony Orchestra. Philip Farkas, a great horn player, was the principal first horn and I was his assistant. One of my duties as an assistant in the orchestra was to play first horn in the Children's Concerts. There was usually one rehearsal for each of the concerts, and it was at one of the first concerts that I was confronted with Friedrich von Flowtow's overture to his opera "Martha," which has an extended horn solo. The performance was a devastating experience for me because I became nervous; I did not miss any notes, but my tone shook. It was not an impressive showing for those wonderful musicians in the Chicago Symphony. I felt terrible because I had let them down. I realized something was basically wrong with my playing technique. Several of my friends in the orchestra recommended that I speak to Arnold Jacobs, and he agreed to help.

The first 10 lessons were concerned with the physical application of breathing. They were like going to a gymnasium and performing physical exercises, most of them relating to breathing. I hardly ever played a note on my horn; my primer was a book on yoga breathing.

The next group of lessons dealt with long tones and their application to the development of breath control. Many of these studies were acquired by Mr. Jacobs during his student days at the Curtis

94

Institute of Music in Philadelphia. Long tones and all the variations of dynamic color were part of my diet, and I have used these ideas in my own teaching with excellent results.

This was a traumatic period for me. It was difficult for me to negotiate changes in embouchure while still trying to fulfill my obligations in the orchestra. I would be exhausted after a long afternoon with Mr. Jacobs and then have to return in the evening for an arduous concert. Lessons sometimes lasted two or more hours. Mr. Jacobs was not your typical clock-watching teacher; rather, it was a case of a stubborn student resisting a more stubborn and determined teacher. He was tough, demanding, and firm. Arnold Jacobs is an even-tempered man, not easily upset by the failure of his students to achieve results; but I also remember the times when he became impatient and exasperated with me. He was not gentle with me in those moments when I deserved to play better, but in the heat of battle, we both won the war.

I can never repay him for his help. He is a great teacher because he not only understands the physical and emotional implications of performing, he also analyzes the problems caused by the personality in question. His success as a remedial specialist among professional performing instrumentalists is legion.

I was fortunate to be in one of the great orchestras in the world, sitting next to Philip Farkas, my ideal as a horn player, and being watched over by Arnold Jacobs on a daily basis. Jacobs encouraged me to study voice, which was of great help in developing my musicianship and musical interpretation. Years later we renewed our professional ties by playing in several summer camp organizations. On one of these he was the featured soloist performing the Strauss Horn Concerto No. 1 transcribed for tuba. It was a remarkable performance of technique and musicianship.

There are many great performing instrumentalists in our symphony orchestras. Arnold Jacobs is one of these. As a knowledgeable teacher he may have no peer for his accomplishments with all students of the brass family. I am proud to have been associated with Arnold Jacobs as a musical colleague, and I am forever indebted to him for his personal help as a teacher and friend.

Steven Zellmer
Trombone, Minnesota Orchestra

The Arnold Jacobs legacy began for me in 1947; I had moved to Chicago after the war to begin school, and in the fall I joined the Chicago Civic Orchestra. From that time on the Chicago Symphony trombone-tuba section became a strong influence and inspiration for me. In addition to its own rehearsals and concerts, the Civic Orchestra training included attendance at Chicago Symphony rehearsals and concerts and section rehearsals coached by Frank Crisafulli. I had also begun private study with Edward Kleinhammer, so my association with the Chicago Symphony musicians was quite involved.

Arnold Jacobs' influence on me began indirectly through the study I did with Frank Crisafulli and Edward Kleinhammer, both of whom had worked with him. Also, my contact with Arnold's students who were in the Civic Orchestra inevitably led to discussions of his ideas and attendance of many Chicago Symphony rehearsals and concerts. Hearing Jacobs at these concerts made a strong impression on me.

I was first introduced to Arnold by Paul Walton, his tuba student and friend. From that time on Arnold always recognized and greeted me. I also was hired as an extra player with the Chicago Symphony during this time and had chances to talk with him then. Arnold's outgoing personality and willingness to communicate made him easy to approach. Students and others often engaged him in conversations about brass playing; he discussed his ideas freely, with the zeal of a missionary, which is what I think he has always been. His true genius was displayed by complete involvement in his material and the mastery of his instrument. He brought new clarity to the fundamentals of brass playing with a method that could be called scientific if you were careful not to overlook the fact that, while his fundamentals were indispensable, they were always presented as a means to better serve the music and never as an end in themselves.

By 1951 Arnold had already developed a reputation as a great teacher as well as great player. His tuba students were playing in the Kansas City, Pittsburgh, and Minneapolis Symphonies and trombone players and others were also studying with him. My private study with him began early in 1952. I can remember the first of many trips to his house on the south side of Chicago; from the Loop I had to take the Illinois Central to 87th Street and from there transfer to a bus to Normal Street, which left a couple of blocks to walk. As I approached his house I knew he was home if his Lincoln was parked in front, and I could usually hear tuba or trombone playing coming from his basement. Once I rang the doorbell there was always a commotion of welcome from his dog and once inside, I was greeted by his wife, Gizella, and his mother-in-law. If he was still working, students waited in the living room with the tropical fish or were invited to the dining room table for coffee. When Arnold came up from his studio he was always relaxed and in a good mood, looking forward to the next lesson. He worked hard, but I never heard him complain, and I never heard him say anything but positive things about his work and about others, with the exception of an occasional remark about a conductor who didn't measure up.

Once I went down to the studio it was all business, with concentrated discussions and demonstrations. At the first lesson I was impressed that rather simple material took on a new importance when I tried to play it with the kind of sound he wanted. He talked about the sensations that accompany a good sound and suggested that I look for these sensations when I heard the right sound. I inevitably left the lessons with important new ideas I couldn't wait to start working on. Almost from the first lesson, I started to develop a new confidence based on understanding of what I was doing.

During this time I worked in a record store a block from Orchestra Hall. Just as I was leaving for a lesson one day, the new Mercury recording of Pictures at an Exhibition with Kubelik came in. It had been recorded on April 23, 1951 and marked the beginning of the High-Fi era. Arnold had played the Bydlo solo on a C tuba, which gave it an especially heavy and appropriate sound; we had all been thrilled to hear him play it during the Orchestra Hall concerts. As soon as I gave him the record he wanted to hear it; as I remember he wasn't too happy with it because he felt the best take hadn't been used. Anyone who has recorded has probably experienced this frustration.

In the fall of 1952 I joined the Indianapolis Symphony, and as soon as the season ended I returned to Chicago to study again.

With Arnold's recommendation and support I was offered the Grant Park Symphony for the summer of 1953. After another season in Indianapolis and my return to Chicago in the spring of 1954, a great opportunity opened up for me; I had just finished a lesson and was walking down Normal Street when Arnold drove up and excitedly called out that he had just gotten a call from Minneapolis; they wanted me to come up as soon as possible to audition for a first trombone opening. Earlier in the year Antal Dorati had guest conducted in Chicago and Arnold talked to him about me. Dorati was interested because he had already hired two of Arnold's students, Paul Walton, tuba, and Eugene Isaeff, bass trombone, both of whom he liked. I was on the first plane to Minneapolis and, after a sleepless night at the Curtis Hotel, I auditioned the following afternoon. Several days later I was offered the job, and I believe it was Arnold's support and encouragement that made it possible for me.

After joining the Minneapolis Symphony in the fall of 1954, I returned to Chicago for the next seven summers to play with the Grant Park Symphony. During those times I was able to take some lessons and I also had opportunities to play extra at Ravinia. I remember one occasion when I drove to Ravinia with Arnold, and we didn't arrive until about 10 minutes before the rehearsal began. I remarked that I often didn't get to rehearsals much earlier in Minneapolis, and he said it was a good sign that I didn't need a lot of warm-up.

A highlight for me during those summers in Chicago was an annual get-together with the Jacobs. I especially remember a party at the Shelbyrne Hotel when I introduced my wife to them. Rita immediately felt the warmth of both Gizella and Arnold, and from then on she, too, looked forward to seeing them each year. I remember that Arnold sometimes discussed his ideas over the dinner table and, even as a layman, my wife said she found them fascinating.

I was first made aware of a side of Arnold that few people knew when I went to Indianapolis, where Louie Ruth, a trumpet player, who had also been there when Arnold played in Indianapolis, told me that Arnold was able to drink more beer at that time than anyone he had ever known. I guess I should have remembered that when we invited the Jacobs to dinner in the summer of 1961, my last in Chicago. We drank a great deal of wine, followed by Galliano, and the evening ended up with me having to go to bed before anyone left. The next morning I asked my wife what had happened, as I could only remember the embarrassment. Arnold didn't seem to have any trouble, so I would have to acknowledge him as the master there, too.

Since 1961 I have had few opportunities to see Arnold, but friends pass on news about him. My own recollections of the times I spent in Chicago and my studies with him are happy and cherished memories. If I have done any good playing over the past 30 years I am sure Arnold's influence had something to do with it.

Chicago Symphony Brass Quintet plus one in 1951. Left to right, Ron Hasselmann, Renold Schilke, Arnold Jacobs, Adolph Herseth, Frank Crisafulli, and Hugh Cowden.

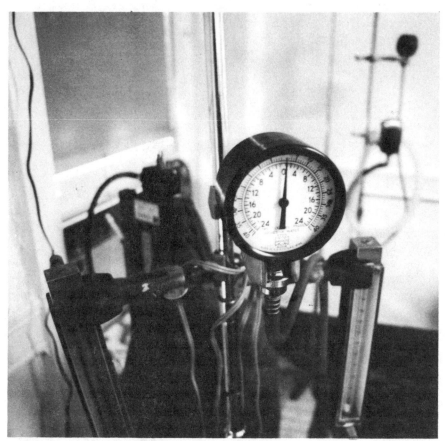

Rich Mays

From Arnold Jacobs' studio

Epilogue

Those acquainted with Arnold Jacobs have little reluctance in stating their feelings about him. Obviously the contributors to this collection feel that the training and association they have had with Mr. Jacobs dramatically shaped their lives and careers. It is easy for me to understand this feeling because as I read the letters and articles that evolved into this book, I relived many events in my own development. No one who has had the opportunity will ever forget the basement at 8839 South Normal, the kindness of Mrs. Jacobs, the sound of Mr. Jacobs' voice (even over the telephone), and the necessity to rush from the lesson to the car to write down as many ideas and facts as could be remembered. The Jacobs studio is famous for its large array of unforgettable training aids. Mr. Jacobs' extensive knowledge and intuitive skills allow him to use equipment in a manner that is far removed from gimmickry.

Some areas of study that have been of greatest importance to me are the sense of resonance; the feeling of the sound in the face and the sensations of the vibrations in the hands as they hold the instrument; how this can be most easily obtained by modeling the sound of Jacobs' instrument or voice; the free, unencumbered breath; the open, relaxed throat; feeling the cold air deep in the throat; making music always; and the use of mouthpiece and rim buzzing. These are the hallmarks of my study with Arnold Jacobs.

Mouthpiece buzzing has been important to me in performing and teaching. After returning from my first lesson with Arnold Jacobs, I buzzed my mouthpiece in a rehearsal and my girlfriend (who was later to become my wife) remarked, "What a horrible sound." It may not sound pretty, but it certainly is a strong pedagogical technique.

Although I have not studied formally with Arnold Jacobs for many years, the strength of my training is evident in my performance and pedagogy on a daily basis. Equally important is his availability as a friend and guide. His counseling is of the greatest value to me and will never be forgotten.

101

Preparation of this document encompassed several years, but its development was a constant source of stimulation. I received many anxious letters and telephone calls from contributors during this time. The care and concern they took in writing about ideas, facts, and concepts is illustrated in their articles. This contact with so many musicians reinforced my own early studies in a positive way. The many conversations I had with Mr. Jacobs during this time were also quite interesting. The successes of those he has worked with make him proud, of course, but he also showed a great interest in their nonmusical lives. Frequently, he discussed hobbies, family, or some other unique aspect about the individual. It could well be that these other areas of our lives have also been affected by the association with Arnold Jacobs.

Often when calling for Mr. Jacobs, he would not be home and I would speak with Mrs. Jacobs. On one such occasion, I asked how Mr. Jacobs was feeling and she said, "He is 70 years old, you know. I know how that feels because I am 75!" I suppose I showed some surprise at this new tidbit of information and she proceeded to tell me how she learned that she was five years his senior. Mrs. Jacobs said that during all the preparations for their marriage (license application, medical testing, and so on), she had made no notice of his age. Shortly after the ceremony they drove from Chicago to Philadelphia to visit his family. Driving through the Allegheny Mountains, they came to a scenic overlook and decided to stop. Mr. Jacobs turned to her and indicated that he had something very important that he must tell her before she met his family. She said she was quite alarmed and the first thing that came to her mind was that he must have another wife someplace! He then informed her that he was just 20 years old; she was 25. Mrs. Jacobs laughed as she remembered how relieved she was and said, "He was always so mature and handsome!" Mr. Jacobs later spoke about this and said that the age difference has been an asset of increasing value. Their marriage certainly appears to be a partnership of quality.

We were especially proud of Mrs. Jacobs during the "block-busting" times of the 1950s. She appeared on the cover of the *Saturday Evening Post* standing on her porch with some of her friends behind a sign reading, "This house not for sale."

Arnold Jacobs' intellect and ease of sharing have been an influence on generations of musicians, a legacy that has changed our world. I trust that this collection is enjoyable and of value to the reader; its preparation was a wonderful experience. Many thanks to all the friends who agonized and labored in love over their manuscripts with the intensity of performing in Carnegie Hall. It seems appropriate to sum it all up with the first and last statements from the contributors: "Arnold Jacobs is a phenomenon that I'm glad happened to me during my lifetime." "If I have done any good playing . . . I am sure Arnold's influence had something to do with it." Arnold Jacobs, we thank you!

M. Dee Stewart

The Dynamics of Breathing
by Kevin Kelly
with Arnold Jacobs and David Cugell, M.D.

At some time every student of a wind instrument is instructed in the "correct" method of breathing. If he studies with two or three different teachers, he probably learns two or three different methods, all presumably correct. I studied with six horn teachers and learned five breathing methods, each slightly different and none especially helpful.

The problem is two-fold. First, few teachers fully understand how the body regulates breathing, let alone how the breath is used in wind instrument playing. Second, those who have at least a partial understanding teach it in the wrong way, through attention to anatomy. The teacher's incomplete understanding is conveyed to the student, who becomes confused, disillusioned, perhaps even immobilized. The standard "art of playing" books for each instrument help little, because few are coherent on the subject and even fewer agree with any other text.

In an attempt to understand this problem, I conferred with two noted authorities on the subject of breathing: Dr. David W. Cugell, Bazley Professor of Pulmonary Diseases at the Northwestern University Medical School in Chicago, who also heads the Pulmonary Function Laboratory at Northwestern Memorial Hospital; and Arnold Jacobs, principal tubist of the Chicago Symphony Orchestra and a world-renowned teacher, who is sought by students and professionals on all wind instruments, primarily for his approach to the psychology of breathing.

Wind instrument players are concerned with the creation and maintenance of a moving column of air, which is the responsibility of the respiratory muscles alone. Many of the muscles of the abdomen and chest, and some in the neck, are involved in moving air in and out of the lungs. The diaphragm is the one most frequently mentioned in connection with wind instrument playing

This article is reprinted from the December 1983 issue of *The Instrumentalist* and the one least understood by wind players. It is popularly considered a main element in the concept of breath "support" — we are often told to support the tone from the diaphragm — as if the diaphragm were active in expiration (blowing air out). It is not.

"The diaphragm is a muscle of inspiration (taking air in)," Cugell says. "Located around and above the abdomen (see example 1), it is unique among the muscles of the body in that it contracts not from one end to the other, as the muscles in your arm, leg, or back would, but in a circular fashion, so that a contraction of the diaphragm will reduce its size while flattening it out. The diaphragm is connected to the lower ribs in such a manner that when it contracts it moves downward. It's one muscle, but like all muscles it's made up of multiple fibers that contract synchronously. When it contracts, the effect is to push it downward.

"The active part of breathing is the inspiratory portion. In order to move air into the chest and expand the lungs, an active muscle effort is required, and that means contraction of the diaphragm. Now you can produce a little bit of breathing by contracting other muscles, such as the strap muscles in the neck. You see someone complete a hundred-yard dash, they're gasping and tugging with their neck muscles as well as with their diaphragm, but that's the agonal gasp of the subject who is in extremes of physical activity, which is not the case when you're playing a musical instrument. You may need to breathe in a hurry or you may need a big breath, but coordinated and planned breathing is not assisted by contracting some of these other muscles, which contribute relatively little in comparison with what a healthy diaphragm can do."

Cugall points out that the diaphragm functions only to assist taking the air in. "It's the other muscles, particularly in the chest area and the abdomen, that we use to exhale and that collectively develop the air pressure you need to play.

"A man in England did a nice little study in which he had a number of trained si igers stand in front of a fluoroscope (an instrument used to examine the interior of a body) and told them to sustain a note with the breath coming from the diaphragm in whatever manner they were trained. Then he repeated the process and had the singers breathe in a manner which was quite incorrect, without using the diaphragm in the way in which they had been instructed. The fluoroscope showed no difference whatsoever in the activity of the diaphragm under these two circumstances. This is really not surprising, because the diaphragm accounts for

105

90% of all breathing and you cannot control or change the proportion of your breathing that is contributed by it (or by a few other muscles, whose contribution is relatively small).

"Now what I suspect is happening is that when someone sustains a high C in a proper way 'using the diaphragm' — as opposed to someone who does it improperly — it has not really anything to do with the diaphragm. It has to do with how the person contracts other muscles in the abdomen and chest. This information has been transferred in the lingo of singers and wind instrument players to assume that this exhaling is accomplished with the diaphragm, when in fact it is done by contracting other muscles.

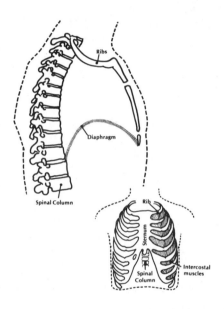

Example 1 The diaphragm is connected to the lower ribs and contracts in a circular fashion as it moves downward.

"There are two overlapping layers of muscles between the ribs, called the intercostal muscles; some contract during inspiration and some contract during expiration. If I inhale in a hurry and I want to stop at a certain point, before I actually stop, the muscles which move the chest in the opposite direction begin to work. It is this interplay of the muscles that moves things in opposite directions which provides the fine control."

106

The late Professor Arend Bouhuys, of the Yale University School of Medicine, to whom Cugell referred to frequently in our discussions, offers a good illustration of how the breathing-in and breathing-out muscles cooperate in wind playing:

The respiratory muscles help to generate most of the energy that goes into playing a horn. They act on the chest, which is for our purposes an elastic bellows. When the chest (that is, the lungs in it) is full of air, the chest tends to collapse as it relaxes. Just try for yourself: inhale as far as you can, relax all muscles, and you exhale with a sigh. Now try the opposite, which is more difficult to do: breathe about as far as you can. Now relax all muscles, and the air flows in. The resting position of the chest bellows is somewhere in between, roughly in the middle of the volume excursion range of the chest. The respiratory muscles have to work with or against these elastic forces, depending on what the chest volume is and what pressure we need to play the horn.

If we first want to breathe out slowly with very little pressure, after breathing in as far as possible we must use considerable inspiratory force to keep the air from going out with a sigh. Again, try for yourself. Breathe in deeply, and let go very slowly. You have to 'brake' your exhaling, using inspiratory muscles to hold back, to keep the chest volume from decreasing too rapidly because of its own elasticity. When you continue, you reach a point where you are relaxed. Now continue to breathe out slowly, and you find that you now have to push with expiratory muscles to move the air out at the same slow rate. (Arend Bouhuys, "Physiology and Musical Instruments." Reprinted by permission from *Nature*, volume 221, number 5187, page 1200. Copyright ©1969, Macmillan Journals, Ltd.)

The amount of control the wind instrument player has over this procedure is limited by what is called the pressure-volume diagram of the chest (example 2), which says that greater pressure is required to move air at volumes below the resting lung volume than at volumes above the resting point. As Cugell explained it, "In the lung the pressure-volume relationship is linear over the midrange — that is, I get equal volume increments for equal pressure increments. Once I reach the elastic limit, no matter how much pressure I apply, I don't get any more volume.

Example 2

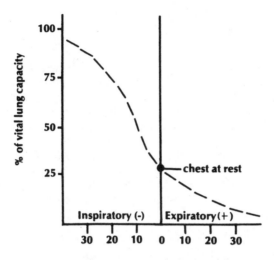

During slow release of a breath, inspiratory muscles (*not* including the diaphragm) keep chest high. Below the chest resting point, expiratory muscles further reduce lung size as moving the air becomes more difficult.

"With no conscious effort to facilitate things, the pressure is greatest when the lungs are largest. Similarly, when the lungs are largest, the conscious contraction of the muscles produces the highest pressures. Active expiratory effort is, of course, needed whenever the required mouth pressure for the instrument is higher than the relaxation pressure at the prevailing lung volume. As the lungs get smaller, they are no longer going to contract and generate pressures on their own. You have to do it by squeezing with the muscles.

"For example, if you inflate the lungs to their absolute maximum and then play a high C on the trumpet at maximum volume, you haven't used much air, but the volume of air in the chest is reduced considerably because you've had to squeeze so much. You compress the air in the chest just as much as the air in the mouth. Whether you have an instrument that has a low pressure, for

108

which you're going to need a high air flow to get a large sound volume, or you're playing an instrument that has a low flow at enormous pressure (one that uses a small mouthpiece) the effort required of the player is essentially the same. In other words, you've got to squeeze with the muscles to generate either a high flow or a high pressure.

The vast difference is that if you don't need much pressure you can play with the entire usable portion of the lung volume. However, if you need a lot of pressure you can only use a small portion of the lung capacity because when the lungs are partially empty it's not possible to generate the pressure, as shown in example 2. You can generate the maximum pressures when the lungs are full, and you want to do that to play a loud, high note; but after you've exhaled some air the lungs are smaller and then it's not possible to sustain as high a pressure. So there is a limited period of time when a player has both the volume and the pressures to produce the sound. On the other hand, the time during which an oboist can sustain a note is not limited so much by the air pressure and air flow requirements of the instrument as by his breath-holding time. If you don't need much pressure and you don't need much flow, then you've got all day; but there's only so long you can hold on before you've got to breathe again."

The point that Cugell insisted upon throughout our discussions is that, given all the facts of breathing anatomy, each player will discover the practical applications for himself: "I'm a firm believer in the capacity of the organism to minimize the burden of the work it has to achieve. In other words, there are studies that show whatever breathing pattern people assume generally represents the minimum amount of work that is required to produce the necessary amount of breathing.

"For example, people with a certain kind of lung disease breathe with a large breath relatively slowly. When making objective measurements of the work of breathing — and by that I mean the pressure, the volume, the physical parameters of work — you will find that if you change their breathing so that they are breathing with a smaller volume more frequently, which would net out to the same amount of breathing, the work required is larger. A patient who has the kind of lung disease that makes the lung stiff may adopt a breathing pattern of panting. He does that because it takes a lot of work to distend a stiff lung. The patient can breathe the necessary amount if he breathes quickly and at small volumes. If you tell him, 'Gee, you're breathing all wrong. Try taking a big breath and breathe less frequently, you'll get the same amount of breathing for it,' he'll say, 'Well I tried it and I didn't like it,' because he had to work so hard to expand the stiff lung.

"My point is that the compensatory pattern of breathing that people spontaneously adopt will represent the minimum work that is required, and it is probably incorrect to impose a different pattern. I think a person playing a wind instrument fits into the same category. If he's got to grab a breath between two passages, he's going to do it in a way that's best for him; I doubt that there would be any purpose in imposing a different pattern. If the player did it once and ran out of air, the next time he's going to breathe a little more because he knows he has to."

Furthermore, the particular breathing pattern a person adopts is no indication of his quality as a wind instrument player. Cugell says. "If you compare the breathing patterns of you and me or anybody else, they would all be different, but there would be no way to categorize that as saying 'normal' or 'abnormal' or 'this one's old' or 'this one's young.' There's nothing characteristic about breathing that can be defined as representing gradations of normality. That being the case, it's not surprising that if four people play the same music, they're going to breathe a little differently, because they breathe differently when they're not playing music."

He referred to the *Nature* article, where Bouhuys tested four flutists playing Debussy's *Syrinx*. One of these men was first chair in the Concertgebouw Orchestra of Amsterdam, one was a good amateur, and two were young professionals. Recordings from a pneumograph (an instrument designed to measure chest movement during respiration) showed four slightly divergent readings within the same general pattern, with slight tempo fluctuations. With the exception of one man, who had a slightly smaller lung capacity and took one extra breath, the performers adhered to the phrase-breath markings in the music. This test showed to what extent the music determines a player's breathing pattern. "So if we subscribe to the concept, with respect to instrument playing, that we will spontaneously assume the most efficient and effective pattern," says Cugell, "then it certainly makes good sense not to concern yourself with it so you can concentrate on all the other aspects of your playing."

110

Anatomy and Psychology

Arnold Jacobs bases his teaching on all these other aspects of sound and phrase — the "products" of music. He makes the distinction between anatomy and function through what he calls the "computer activity of the brain," separate from the "thinking part of the brain."

"When you go to the product of whatever you're trying to accomplish, you'll find the physical action required to do it is based in the computer activity of the brain. In other words the conscious levels of the brain, where volitional thought takes place, handle the product. Another level of the brain, the thinking part, will handle motor impulses carried by nerves throughout the body. The firing up of the systems is handled at subconscious levels, just like the ability to walk or to talk or to run. The muscle activity will result from what you're trying to accomplish. With all machines there is a set of controls, like an automobile, which has complex machinery under the hood but simple controls in the driver's compartment. There's nothing as complex on this planet as the human being; but man has magnificent controls, and he goes through this control system.

"By this I mean that there are divisions in the brain that are going to control all sorts of physical functions — cutting up food, bringing it to the mouth and chewing it, handling the body for sleep at night, or even going insane. The thinking part of the brain is free to cope with life around us. It's with the thinking part of the brain that we begin to establish what we want in the way of product.

"This, of course, is what players are up against; in music so often a teacher makes the mistake of altering the machine activity rather than altering the product or what he wants accomplished. The instructor is giving machine methods of how to do it, and people can't work that way. None of us can. We have to look for the easy answer all the time. It is so simple. If you want a lot of breath, just take a lot of air. Don't worry about where it goes. If you want to blow, just blow. With students a teacher should always try for the simple answers that bring about proper motor response. That idea belongs not in the realm of anatomy but in psychology."

The answer that Jacobs introduces students to is what he calls the "phenomenon of wind" — the idea of air blowing out through the instrument to prevent pressures from building up inside the

111

lungs. Most students who come to Jacobs have acquired the habits of thinking about air pressure instead of air in motion. Because these habits are difficult to break, he uses psychology to create new habits, to get students to use their muscles for the proper function.

The respiratory muscles are involved in three ways. One is respiration, the single complete act of breathing in and out. The second has to do with pelvic pressures when the upper end of the airway is closed, forcing pressure downward for such events as defecation and childbirth. The third has to do with the isometrics of physical function, the kind of static muscle tightening involved in weight-lifting and wrestling.

"A musician has to make sure that he is using the right approach when playing an instrument," Jacobs says. "He doesn't want the one that immobilizes, he doesn't want the one that creates great isometric contractions that have no movement potential. Because a continuous flow of air requires movement, the player should go to respiration.

"The human brain is responsible for conditioned responses to stimuli or reflex responses to stimuli in everybody, musicians or non-musicians. These are non-respiratory functions. In respiration a bellows action occurs in the muscles. We take air in and we blow air out by the phenomena of enlargement and reduction. It becomes simple when you think of movements of air. Whether it's from the diaphragm descending or the rib cage ascending, there has to be enlargement to lower air pressure internally below atmospheric pressure so air will move into the lungs. The same thing happens as you reduce the size — the air pressure increases as you move out. That's how we blow; it's how we breathe.

Move Air As Wind

"The psychology of blowing is always to blow outward, to work with wind rather than air pressure. The psychology of it is important. Take your hand, hold it at a distance and blow onto it. Now where the air lands is the area to concentrate on. Some teachers will have the player blow through the instrument or through the far wall. It doesn't matter what the technique is to motivate a student; the psychology of it is to move air as wind, not air pressure.

"With wind there is always air pressure. With air pressure, there is not always wind. If you just concentrate on the air pressure — which can happen in any body cavity — the danger is that you may have stimulated the Valsalva maneuver (in which you try to

112

breathe out with your mouth and nose shut) or the pelvic pressure syndrome, or the isometrics, which do not involve movements of air.

"But an instructor is never going to get this idea across by telling students to push with this muscle or that muscle. I get them to blow. Away from the instrument I let them observe their body. I use special equipment or I may have students blow up balloons or blow out matches, and then show how quantities can be taken from any part of the thorax (the body area between the neck and the abdomen). In other words we go through a certain amount of perspective training away from music to become acquainted with the body, so that the studies of air in life are involved."

The confusion of many teachers about both the role of the diaphragm and the idea of abdominal "support" of air is largely responsible for many students' preoccupation with the kind of pressures resulting from misdirected muscular tensions.

"First of all, the term 'support' raises questions in itself. Many people make the mistake of assuming the muscle contraction is what gives support. The blowing of the breath should be the support, not tension in the muscles of the body, but the movement of air as required by the embouchure or the reed.

"You go into the mechanics of movement and confusion arises; it's a cause and effect relationship. When a player blows, the body undergoes certain changes. There will be increasing palpable tensions that can be felt just by touching a person. Toward the end of a breath there will be a certain number of fibers that are stimulated. There will be increasing motor activity in order to get the air out, and this varies according to the length of the phrase and the amount of air in the lungs originally; but 'support' is never 'tight muscles,' whether you're silent or blowing, or in a *diminuendo* or *crescendo*. In other words it's simply a static, constant, isometric type of contraction that so many people call support. This is not support at all.

"I can explain it from different points of view. Do it this way: your diaphragm is like the floor, a movable partition between the thoracic and the abdominal cavities. Now if you were to build up considerable air pressure with a loose abdomen and a loose diaphragm, the air would simply move the floor downward. Instead of air coming out, as the player builds pressure it would simply lower the floor. So by thinking of support as something that will hold the diaphragm in the upper position, you could conceivably see abdominal tension as building pressure beneath the floor. You keep that in a fixed position while building up high pressure through the rib activity to have expulsion of breath based on this pressure. I can't conceive of it this way, but I know that many teachers think this way. This is not, to me, support.

"Support is always a reduction phenomenon. Wherever the player is going to build pressure, according to Boyle's Law, he is going to have a reduced chamber. Now the chamber can be reduced anywhere it is enlarged. It gets bigger when you take air in, it gets smaller when you move air out. When you blow, the brain will deactivate the diaphragm, normally. Expiratory function will normally deactivate inspiratory function. If you are using air to create pelvic pressures, the diaphragm will not deactivate — it will remain stimulated. Abdominal muscles that would normally be expiratory will start contracting, and there will be a closure at the throat or the tongue or the lips which causes the air pressure to bear down on a downward-contracting diaphragm to increase the pelvic pressure for expulsion of fecal matter. Of course, to bypass this we have to have a blowing phenomenon that is different. You see, you have to form a new habit, and a new habit does not come right away. A new habit takes time to reach the subconscious level."

Jacobs uses a wide variety of non-musical exercises to get players to feel and hear the difference between blowing air out freely and blowing out in a choked manner that results in tight chest and abdominal muscles. For example, blow onto the back of the hand using a tight hissing sound through your teeth, as loud as possible. You will feel very little air. By blowing out freely onto the hand, you feel a considerable amount of air under low pressure. The hiss is under high pressure, but there is little quantity. By closing the lips in the midst of the hiss and then releasing the sound explosively, you will have felt considerable pressure behind the lips and also behind the tongue. As soon as you open the lips, you have an immediate shortage of air.

"We see these closures in students all the time," Jacobs says, "coming from a sibilant 's' (the hissing sound) or at the back of the tongue, and even some where the larynx and epiglottis start to come together. If I have a student whose tongue is blocking the air, allowing very little air movement but at high pressure, I immediately encourage using the open vowel form such as 'oh' or 'ah.' All through life you have language; language involves the tongue. Over the years you have built up reflex response for shape that is very powerful. You hear a trumpet or a bassoon, but it sounds like a singer with a voice like that singing 'oh.' Listen for that sound and the tongue shape is correct. This pertains to any need to open up the airway."

Following one of Jacobs' recent master classes at Northwestern University, a woman asked how to help a bassoon student who lets the air get "like a brick wall" — constricted and tense — which apparently resulted in quite a horrible sound.

"First of all," he said, "get her away from the bassoon. You don't have to use the reed; just put something in her mouth. Have the student start blowing or start blowing against something in order to see that the air will do something where it lands. The importance of this approach is not to correct what's wrong, but to establish what should be right.

"I would give her a couple of straws and have her blow at the pages of a book and watch what happens on the other side. Have her blow at some matches or blow up a weak balloon, but always with the thought of becoming acquainted with air, rather than air pressure. Studying childbirth and coughing gives the picture of what air pressure will do. However, when you study a burn and cool it by blowing on the hand, or when you're doing what I used to do, blow peas at people with a pea shooter, then you get a different picture of what air will do."

The woman pointed out that this particular student was a singer who had played the bassoon for only a year. "Don't singers have to use a lot of air?" she asked.

"No, it's just the opposite," Jacobs said. "Singers use less air than anybody. Their reed is at the throat, and as a result they have to keep a fairly sizable pressure at the laryngeal region. The student is using the technique of singing on the bassoon. Now compared to singing, bassoon playing will seem like a large volume of air is in transit. It's important to recognize that she has habits already formed.

"Start mechanical movements without the instrument so the student experiences change in the abdominal-diaphragmatic relationship. Deliberately have her create massive motions in the abdominal region, sucking the belly in, forcing it out, pushing it up and down — this is the region where she's been stabilized. Now deliberately destabilize it. Start the muscle activity of change in front of a mirror so the senses work together to strengthen each other.

115

Don't tie it into music, though, or else she'll have to fight her own habits.

"Then tie in the movements of air by using motion — every day — blowing out matches, taking in lots of air and enlarging. Allow a few weeks, where she has to be practicing this every day. In the abdominal region where the student was stable, she will begin to establish motility of function. It has to be recognized in this manner before you apply it to the bassoon. Then you do it with just some reed squawks, but with exaggeration.

"Exaggeration is one of the important tools. Doing things just right is not what you want. The recognition is not there. So you overchange. You're not doing it with the music, so there's no damage. Then when you get to the bassoon, you don't worry about the body change, but you go to the study of air.

"It is natural for the lungs to get smaller as you use up air. The bassoon student has made it unnatural. As a teacher, you go through a program to get her back to what is natural. As soon as this process starts, she begins to use air as wind to deactivate the diaphragm. There can be no stiffness in the anterior abdominal wall without the antagonist, which is the diaphragm. The brain will deactivate this action, and as the diaphragm comes up, you'll find the student is able to blow against the reed, where the wind belongs. If you tell her to do these things based on intelligence, she will understand, but she can't communicate it to her body. The wind becomes the body's signal for change.

It's the Tone
"But wind is finally only a minor part. Tone production is the major. You use the wind as fuel. With a wind instrument, the horn resonates sound waves; it's reacting to sound and amplifying it according to acoustical properties. Our air isn't used to fill an instrument. It's used by the embouchure as energy so the lips vibrate.

"So players certainly shouldn't worry about the air, but about the quality of tone. When you get the tone, you will have all the requirements of tone at the subconscious levels. The blowing is an incidental part; the tone doesn't exist without the blowing, but the blowing can exist without the tone. As an artist you go for the product — the product is sound and phrase and all the emotions in music — you use thought processes that stimulate motor function, but you don't worry about the function. You worry about the sound. You will use the breath as needed. You will do it primarily

116

without awareness of air. The air should be used freely — waste it, do anything you want. A players's awareness is of the communication of sound to whoever he is talking to.

"This is true of any wind instrument. You teach expertise in phrase and the study of dynamics. As the sound production becomes more efficient, which it will, you'll find that you use the breath with greater and greater ease. I'm an old man, but I can still function quite well in playing a brass instrument, because my lips respond quite readily to my thoughts. Moving air under pressure is required for my lips to vibrate, but those lips are not trying to resist the air. They're trying to vibrate based on the thoughts coming from my brain in terms of sounds."

There are, of course, many ways students and professionals have of inhibiting their ability to express sound freely. Probably the most common is poor posture. "Posture is very important," Jacobs acknowledges. "We're structured so that the maximal use of air comes in the standing posture, as if you would run or fight for your life. Standing offers the greatest ability to move large volumes of air in and out of the lungs. The closer you get to the supine, the poorer it becomes.

"If you think of the respiratory system, it should be thought of not as one bellows, but as a series of segmented bellows, depending on your posture. When lying on your back on the floor, you'll find there is little ability to use chest breathing. You will have a marvelous use of diaphragmatic breathing, which is more than enough to sustain life; but the diaphragm isolated from the rest of the rib cage provides a rather small breath. There is no such thing as a full breath without the use of the sternum (the compound ventral bone and cartilage that supports the ribs). If I lean back on the chair and reach over my head, the motion pulls the rib cage up, which is already in the expanded position. That means I can't use it for breathing in or out. If I bend forward over my belly, pressure in the abdominal region under the diaphragm is such that I have great difficulty using diaphragmatic function.

"If you need large volumes of air, you will use the entire respiratory system. If you're playing an instrument that doesn't require much air, you're never going to use a full breath; however you should be able to. Performers have to take sufficient air in to be able to complete phrases. This involves taking in quantities of air based on judgments of how much air will be left at the end of a phrase.

117

"Standing while seated is the best posture because players have the greatest ability to move air in and out of the lungs. However, if you are breathing with comfort, the posture doesn't have to be that way. As long as you are in the upright position, you should have more than enough air. If you're a large person with large lung reserves, posture is not that important; however, people who have small lung volumes must stay upright and make use of whatever nature gave them." (We come back to the point that Cugell made earlier: the body will adopt the most comfortable and effective means of performing whatever task it is given to do.)

"In this art form," Jacobs concludes, "we are dealing in sound. Respiration is made too much of. We need sufficient quantities of fuel that we can use easily — as I say, waste it, it's free — but don't make a big deal out of it. We don't start anything with skill; skill is developed over a period of time in spite of yourself. We have to recognize what we're trying to accomplish; the orders that come from the various parts of the brain must be based on the sound of the instrument. We have to make sure that we don't take the level of the brain at which we have volitional thought and try to take charge of the human machine through its individual components. We can't handle it. You've got to get out of the way and allow your body to function for you. The point is to try to sound great when you play."

Kevin Kelly is completing degrees in music criticism and English writing at Northwestern University, where he has played horn in the major wind performance ensembles.

David Cugell, M.D. is head of the pulmonary function laboratory at Northwestern Memorial Hospital in Chicago and has been a member of the faculty at the Northwestern University Medical School since 1955. A graduate of Yale University and the State University of New York School of Medicine in Brooklyn, Cugell is president of the Chicago Lung Association and their representative/director for the American Lung Association. He was awarded the 1983 Chicago Lung Association medal. A musician as well as a physician, Cugell played clarinet and saxophone through college where he was a member of the marching band.

An Interview with Arnold Jacobs
by Bill Russo

This article consists of portions of an interview (unedited) which was broadcast over radio station WFMT in Chicago. Although it covers only a very small percentage of the vast knowledge Mr. Jacobs has accumulated, it should serve as an introduction to some of the concepts which have made Arnold Jacobs such an outstanding teacher that players from all over the world — including top-level professionals — have made the pilgrimage to the studio in the basement of his south-side Chicago home.

The thing I am most interested in chatting with you about is your teaching — especially in respect to the theories and the technological aspects. To begin, for example, I have heard that you have a machine that measures breath capacity — or pressure?

Well, I have a variety of devices — the one you're probably referring to is a respirometer, which measures both the volume of air that can be moved in and out of the lungs — one of the tests of which is called a "vital capacity test," is a test to see how much air can be moved either in or out of the lungs in a single breath.

How much variation is there?

Just enormous.

Really!

It depends very much on the somatotype of the individual and my medical friends are interested in the health factor, too, which does not involve me. Oh, I've had men come to my studio — just as an example — one trumpet player with one of the major symphony orchestras has a lung capacity of 7 litres — I have measured other trumpet players with as low as 3½ litres lung capacity. [1 litre = 29 ounces]

How does this affect the man's playing?

Well, it's like a long bow or a short bow. On tuba — I have a 4 litre lung capacity. One of my colleagues — a very fine young tuba player — has a 6½ litre lung capacity. I couldn't hope to sustain as

This article is reprinted from the February 1973 issue of *The Instrumentalist.*

long on a single breath as he could. I could play the phrases very nicely, etc., but I must find someplace where I can inhale so that I don't run out of fuel too soon.

What's the difference between instruments? And how much more capacity is required for high and low?

Well, I can talk about this fairly well because I did a research program involving this particular item. The trumpet would use the least amount of breath, but under the greatest amount of pressure of any of the brass instruments. The tuba would be just the reverse. It would use the most in terms of volume of air and flow, but under the least pressure — and it runs to something of this nature on trumpet — in the high range, the flow rate — Mr. Herseth cooperated with me on this particular research — and we found that his flow rates in very high range playing would be very low — say maybe 10 litre flow rate per minute under a pressure of oh, sometimes in excess of a pound and a half to 2 pounds. In his lower range, he might be playing with a flow rate of maybe 25-30 litres per minute, under a pressure of maybe 8 or 10 ounces. Now, on tuba, my inter-oral pressure — in other words, the pressure is measured in the mouth cavity while playing. We use a little tube and just insert it into the mouth while playing, and the pressure is read on a read-out device. My lower pressure goes as low as 2 ounces in general playing, but at the same time, my flow rates may go anywhere from 7 litres per minute playing as softly as I can, to well in excess of 120 litres per minute playing in full volume. Now, Dr. Benjamin Burrows at the University of Chicago, who helped me with these experiments, was helping me graph some of these experiments, putting down on paper and he was rather intrigued with the fact that you could draw one curve for the entire brass family in terms of how much air is used, and how much pressure is used in producing this flow rate on the instruments. We had Mr. Farkas involved in this, Mr. Herseth, Mr. Lambert, and myself on tuba — that's trumpet, trombone, French horn, and tuba. But wherever we played notes that were enharmonic — in other words — the same pitch, even though they were on different instruments — our work efforts and flow rates were practically identical. As an example, when I played a high C at a given dynamic that we were working to, I was using about 6 ounces of inter-oral pressure and about 10 litres flow rate per minute, and in graphing this we found that Mr. Herseth on exactly the same note was using practically identical pressure and flow. On a different note, with Mr. Farkas,

120

again we found that my pressure and his were about the same, flow was about the same — even though we were using different instruments. Our embouchures in coming to a given size and shape had a certain requirement for the breath in terms of pressure and movement.

Can I stop you for just a minute? Because I'm getting lost...
Well, this is a rather complex subject...
The flow rate increases? for lower notes? on a given instrument?
In the brass family, yes, at a given dynamic level, the flow rate is almost invariably greater in the low range compared to the high range.
And the pressure decreases for the lower notes?
Exactly.
But, now when you say that different instruments have the same flow rate and same pressure for a given same note...
Enharmonic, yes.
Say, for C1 — does that mean, then that as the tuba increases its flow rate to 10, the trumpet decreases its flow rate down to 10?
Exactly. As he goes into his *low* range, then the pressure eases off and his flow increases; as I go into my *high* range, my pressure increases and the flow decreases.
Terrific. Now what are the implications of this? There are millions, I can see.
Well, there are many implications, as you say, one — psychologically — those of us who play the tuba must realize that we don't have to work too hard when we play in the high range. I have many students who will go into severe isometric types of contraction states simulating the work effort of the trumpet when he's working in his high range, when actually this is not needed. The contraction states involved are very mild.

The upward range of the trombone and the tuba could be increased considerably?
Well, there is a potential for increasing it, surely, it increases as the writers write for it, and as the players are motivated, they always move into it.
What variations are there in the amount of pressure available?
The human factor enters into this and there are wide variations — I don't know whether to go into all phases of this on a discussion program of this type, because we do run into some very com-

plicated problems that involve pressure relaxation systems and the respiratory apparatus.

Let me ask you this, then — can the litre capacity be changed?

Well, there are natural limitations, but very few people come up to their basic potential.

Right. Now it would seem more obvious to me. Can the pressure be changed? the capacity of the person to get pressure?

Oh, yes, because when you study the systems in a biological sense, the act of coughing involves breath pressure, but it's in a spasmodic state, and this raises the pressures to enormous levels in terms of maybe 6-7 lbs. of inter-thorasic pressure at the start of a cough, but I don't know of anybody who can achieve these pressures on a voluntary static breath pressure test. I have never run into anybody that can come close to this.

What is the key to developing a full use of one's lung capacity — it's not just lungs is it?

Well, it is basically the respiratory apparatus rather than just the definition of lungs. Of course, they are somewhat passive. They have a certain elasticity but they respond to movements of the respiratory system.

So how do you get up to your capacity? If it's 3 litres, how do you get right up to the full?

There again we run into complications. There are complications with having very full lungs; there are complications with having deflated lungs. And, there again — I'll try to keep this simple — psychological motivations are very important in this. When a person takes a breath, if he enlarges his body, he can take a pseudo-inspiratory maneuver and substitute it for a valid one because there is a shape change possible where he is not taking air, he is merely going through the motions hoping to take air. But if he takes in a breath, in other words, if he is motivated to take in air, he will find it fairly easy to take it in; it doesn't take any great strength to do it — in fact, the less strength involved, the better. But when he is motivated — not with the respiratory system, but with air, so that the *mechanics* are played down, the *psychodynamics* are played up. The same thing when you blow. Many players will substitute wild contractile states of musculature, actually to where they are going into isometric contractions —

You mean their body is enlarged. . .their chest has gone out and. . .

Yes, they're just taking muscle after muscle that are antagonistic to each other and putting them into a vigorous opposition, but there is no flow of air. Well, there again, if you blow, you'll move the air out; but if you just contract the body in order to blow, then there is a very good chance you won't move the air.

So, you've got to get the person set — to want to take the air in.

Exactly.

Does he always need the full capacity?

No, in fact it's not wise to take the full capacity unless it is needed. There is a range of efficiency in the pulmonary aspects of this. I usually recommend about an 80% inflation of the vital capacity, and when they're down to about 25% a re-inflation of up to about 75-80%, so that the range of function based on my work would be neither extreme — neither totally deflated nor totally inflated.

But the implication of this that I see from a teaching standpoint are obviously staggering.

Well, you really need to know something about the structure and function of the body. I've been a hobbyist on the structure of the body since the early 1940's and I had no idea at all that this would be helpful in teaching — it's just a hobby; the biological sciences have been intriguing to me ever since I was a little boy. But as I went into the studies I began to realize that there are very definite crossovers — the knowledge of one can help the other field, but I am very much against teaching science, and substituting science for an art form. Always stress the programming of a musician. I may use scientific investigative procedures for my understanding of a student's problems, but when I work with a student I — if there is a problem which has to be worked out in a body sense, I do it away from his instrument. We do it completely away from music until we establish normal activity and then re-apply it to the instrumental function. But when I am working with a man as a musician, I always work with his mind, not his body. And we don't stimulate the mind into asking a question, we stimulate it into issuing a statement, so the motor systems involved take their cue by the art form type of thinking...he has to communicate to an audience, and he has to know what he is going to say to an audience with sounds, so his mind has to be flooded with sound and he has to think in terms of it so that we don't have him finding out what various musculatures are doing. I don't like a large sensory involvement or some aesthetic analysis of tissue in function.

Right. But, nonetheless there is a fantastic technical thing going on here...

Oh, yes

*. . .and what I see you are doing very clearly is taking advantage of it to
further art. You are not going to let it impede art, but it's there, nonetheless.*

Student after student comes to see me very much involved in the
mechanisms of function, but the thinking part of the brain is not
equipped to stimulate this type of function. You have to find the
end products. With a musician, you have to realize that conditioned response demands a study of stimuli and we have to work
with a stimulus. It's like a piano player roll, for a simple explanation, we don't operate the keyboards, we go directly to the roll and
get the function right there and the keyboards will respond.

*But there's an irony here, Arnold, because, by using these technical
devices you can minimize the intellectualization of it, because most brass
players that I know — at least before they came to you — used to talk a
lot about the intellectual concomitant of playing, and I think it hung
them up a lot. They talked about how to breathe and what do do. . .
and most often were in the dark. And it seems to me, from what you're
telling me, that you don't want to talk about it so much, but you can get
some true scientific evaluation about what is going on and then work
from the art — free of some of that jargon that's been going around.*

You see, this is the difference between the student and the
teacher. The student — the one who is learning performance — I
feel must respond to the challenges of his art. The teacher has to
guide him and provides proper stimulation in the various stages of
development; but it's very dangerous for a student to be thinking
in terms of measurement. I understand the subject very well, but
when I go on the stage to either do a solo, or my work with the
Chicago Symphony, I do not think in terms of measurements. I
have 2 tubas — one in the head and one in the hand. The one in
the head is all sound and that's the one I work with. The one in
the hand is a mirror of my thought and I let it be the mirror — in
order to have it that way I have to give it something to reflect!

The study of any art form is the study of the mind — of the individual — the creative thought. But for any musician who plays a
brass instrument it is so important. Your pitch source is part of
your neuromuscular systems, the breath, the motor activities, the
involvements of breath as motor force and function are all part of
you — controlled in one way or another by your nervous system
and your mind. The instrument is made up in a factory. It has
three valves and a potential of over three octaves of range. It is ob-

vious that three valves are not going to give the pitch — the player has to put the pitch into the instrument and have it resonated and, as a result, that means we must obey the acoustical laws that govern the brass instrument. We have to send in a frequency that the tube length can respond to, and it is very important that we psyche this out. The psycho-motor activities are actually based on the psyche and the motor activities following in a sense that we have to think our pitch, we have to think our phrase. We're a story teller except that we use audio without words, but we use coloration and sound and so forth and we have a definite message. It does come from the mind through tissue, through amplification and so forth to the audience.

The fascinating thing here is the contrast and yet reconciliation of the extremely technical with the poetical in your talking about this matter. I mean you are going deeper into the technical than anybody I think ever has in brass playing, and yet on the other hand you constantly emphasize the poetical aspect — the interpretative, the artistic part of it.

Well, when you study the functions, you study it *after* the fact — there is not a creative thought. We can make measurements as to what a man has done. We can find out what muscles are functioning. We can get electro-monographic studies, some of the work efforts of the musculatures. We can find out many things; but we are not able with these tools of measurement to find out what the brain is doing. If you are an actor on the stage it's obvious you know when you communicate to an audience. If you want to visualize a scene that involves rage, the actor has to draw on his experiences that involve rage. He has to hate something at the moment and his face will become livid, his voice will become contorted. There are many physiological changes involved as he goes into the emotional state and the audience will read it out. In any art form, regardless of what it may be, it has to come as a psycho-motor involvement where you deliver a message externally. Now the student who spends years and years in study is going through a sensory type of phenomenon. His senses are gathering all sorts of information to be brought to the brain for evaluation. There is a great danger that this young person is not learning performance — he is actually forming habits of learning — and, as a result, he has no message to deliver. I think in the study of music it is very important to separate the activity of research, in the sense of knowing the mechanisms, with a definite requirement the knowledge that the student has to become an inspired individual — one who is able to think in terms of interpretation, and styles and colors and dynamics and the tools of our art. So really I separate them into two categories in the sense that the read-out devices and so forth and the study of structure are very important; but the motivational factors are really our main tools in teaching.

How much are these educational and philosophic and scientific theories — tools that you work with — being made available? Have you written about this? A brochure, a pamphlet, a book?

No, I've been asked to write. I have lectured on this subject moderately, but I haven't written anything as yet. I have things underway, but you know we are just so busy with the orchestra and then my teaching schedule. I have a constant flow of students from various parts of the country that want to come in for specialized work and that keeps me from writing because I'm so busy.

Lecture given by Arnold Jacobs at the Second International Brass Congress Indiana University, June 4, 1984

At Mr. Jacobs' suggestion, it was decided to include some of his thoughts in Arnold Jacobs: Legacy of a Master. *Two presentations at the Second International Brass Congress were chosen and transcribed verbatim from the video tape. I have taken the liberty of converting some of Mr. Jacobs' conversational style into print. Similarly, it was necessary to delete certain sections. Although the impressive visual and aural advantages are missing, the factual subject matter remains. The intended goal is a readable presentation without distortion of the contents. The following is a portion of a panel discussion on pedagogy chaired by Philip Farkas.*

M. Dee Stewart

Arnold Jacobs: I have maybe some rather peculiar ideas about teaching. For instance, I like instrumentation to augment the human intellect, not to replace it but simply to augment it. The human brain is a magnificent tool. People tend to think in different ways though. They have different forms of excellence. One person may think just beautifully in terms of color, spaciousness, and the perspectives that are so valuable in art. I don't think very well in terms of color and space, but I think very well in terms of recall of sound, recognition of sound, color of sound. I recognize a great deal about that. There are people I know that don't do this so well. They think beautifully in terms of logic. I think they've found through psychological testing that people have abilities in their brain that may not be developed but have the potential of development. One former student of mine came to me at a time when I was very much interested in the psychology of physical function, thoughts that tend to bring about motor responses, and how we use them in music. This young man would have qualified as being tone deaf. When I would sing a note, he could not sing the note. Most of you could immediately respond and reproduce that pitch in whatever octave you like. He could not do that. Finally, I got him to think back to his childhood years in school and he

127

Rich Mays

Jacobs in his studio

finally came up with a crazy little tune something like, "Oh, it ain't gonna rain no more, it ain't gonna rain no more; how in the heck can I wash my neck if it ain't gonna rain no more." It was a very silly little thing that he had learned as a child, and he sang it in tune with all the intervals; everything was fine. It indicated to me that somewhere in that brain there was the ability to have recall of pitch and recognition. In other words, something was interfering with this.

At that time I was interested in augmenting our abilities by bringing more than one sense to bear on a subject. I started this student with the aid of a Stroboconn, (a twelve window job), a tape recorder, and a piano, and we immediately put the instrument down for a while. We started a recognition program of watching a wheel and hearing the pitch at the same time. When the wheel stopped, we knew there was an intonation factor. I didn't ask the student to repeat the pitch after me. I just had him listen in silence, but to have recall in his head, to start a pattern of recognition. We used a tape recorder so that afterwards, whatever pitches were being recorded were actually played back on tape and they could be observed again through the sense of sight, which is one of our very powerful learning senses. We immediately started this program of developing the regions of the brain that have to do with pitch recall. We began to make slow progress, enough to warrant some indication that this was the proper route to take. I admit that in the beginning we used instrumentation to augment his senses because when he would try to think and recall, he would set up a pattern of motor function, but he would lose in the brain what he was trying to actually accomplish as pitch.

If somebody sings a note or plays a note, you have to be able to retain that note in your brain and then you imitate it. You can't let it go from the brain or there's nothing to imitate. When you set up the physical patterns of function and that sound you're trying to imitate has disappeared from the brain, you will actually be unable to reproduce that note. It has to be retained in the brain, and you develop this retention by simply challenging the brain. If a person can't walk, he has to learn to crawl first. But he goes from crawling to walking to running. So we have to start at the level the student can cope with. The young man I have in mind is in one of the professional symphony orchestras today; he has a fine career in music with fine recognition and recall of sound which shows that it can be done.

I feel strongly that when we teach, we must always remember that we're dealing with a human being. We have a student come into the studio and play for us. A teacher has to become sensitive to what the student is like and what he thinks. We must have a message that we impart to a student, but we must also know that he can receive the message. In other words, we must ask if there is a language difficulty. Does the student think along different lines? He may be very intelligent, more so than the teacher, but he may not comprehend because he is not used to verbalizations. He may not be used to the patterns. There are multiple tools that we use to establish two-way communications with students. What I'm very interested in is the fact that when we deal with brass players, we're dealing with a phenomenon that is quite different from the musician who is going to study cello or piano.

When the piano is sent out from the factory, the factory sends out an instrument that has built-in pitch vibration. It has built-in resonance. It requires a motor function. Somebody must provide motor activity or that pitch vibration cannot be achieved. Now I have great respect for pianists. My mother was a marvelous pianist. I love the instrument, it's tremendously difficult, and it requires tremendous development and ability on the part of the human playing the piano. So when I say that you can run a cat down the piano keyboard and you will get sounds, it is not a put-down. It may not be great music, but the factory has sent out an instrument that has already been set up in terms of pitch vibration and resonance. It requires motor function from then on.

We can go to the opposite end of the spectrum — the human voice. Singers have to employ motor functions; they have pitch vibration based on vocal cord activity, and resonance based on the body chambers where the air is going to be resonated and reflected. All three are part of the human being.

The brass player gets an instrument from the factory that has resonance built in, but it does not have built-in pitch vibration or motor function. In other words, out of three basic requirements for sound; pitch vibration, resonance, and motor function, only resonance is built into the brass instrument with its peculiar laws. That means the player must provide the motor activity. This is done through the breath. He has pitch vibration which is done through the vibration of the embouchure. He has resonance according to the partials. The acoustics of the instrument are quite different than the other instruments involved. It's primarily sympathetic resonance. In the piano you have what we call forced resonance. You have one soundboard that resonates all frequencies. You must alter the brass instrument to resonate all frequencies. It has partial laws which must be obeyed.

To bring this into being, the brass player has to be taught so that the dominance in his learning is based on the ability to have recall and conceptual thoughts of sound. There has to be the ability for the vocal cord activity to leave the vocal cords and go to the vocal cords of the trumpet, the embouchure. It has to vibrate according to certain pitch frequencies. This is done by activity in the brain, going down the nerves to reflex activity that is built up in the tissues in the lip. And this is important right from the start. In a pedagogical sense. I'll take a youngster when he comes to my studio and consider him to be an elementary artist — extremely elementary, but he is still in an art form. What I do is take his trumpet and his mouthpiece and I play one note, and make him listen to it. I make him try to absorb the sound of that. I may play it as poorly as I can and make a really atrocious sound. Then I try to play it to the best of my very limited ability and play with a very good sound so the discrimination is started early. I encourage the student to study the sound because he wants to study the instrument. I want him to study the sounds of the instrument so the emphasis is not the physical aspect of playing the trumpet, but the musical aspect of playing the trumpet, horn, trombone, or tuba as a tonal phenomenon.

If I touch this microphone, I use motor systems. There is feedback that comes through a sensory system. We'll always be aware through proprioception of a position of the arm or the hand. We'll get some information back, but the primary functions are motor functions, not sensory. When we play a brass instrument, we are using motor activity primarily. There is a component of sensory feedback, but to communicate to somebody else there has to be psychomotor activity. Tremendously complex things are happening in my body for me to deliver information to you, and I don't know anything about that. What I've learned about this, I've learned by studying other bodies, not my own. In other words, the ability to analyze yourself is extremely limited. You can analyze your products, what you're trying to accomplish in life, you can analyze certain parts of your anatomy where there's more feedback, like in the fingers, proprioception, because we have a nervous system that tells us what's happening in this particular region

131

of our anatomy.

We don't have this in the embouchure. The functions of the embouchure are based primarily on the seventh cranial nerve carrying messages; just like a wiring hookup from a tape recorder. We have a message that comes from the computer activity to the lip where we have developed reflex responses to stimulus. In other words, you don't control the lips, you control the message. In controlling the message, you have controlled the embouchure. The embouchure is not made up of a simple muscular group. It is not your orbicularis oris. It's made up of many groups that feed in to cause the lip to be able to retract, to protract, to elevate, to depress, and to vibrate at different frequencies. This is something that is so enormously complex, the only hope of success is to find a simple answer. The lip must vibrate; that means it has to be motivated to create sound.

When taking a young student, I start them off by demonstrating sound. They want to know how you do it. I don't answer that. I say "try to sound this way; buzz your lips." I will say that and let them buzz on the mouthpiece. "Take the mouthpiece and just make horrible sounds, make musical sounds, do anything you want with it." But they start a pattern of causation, a buzz. Then I ask them to take their trumpet home and play for their father and try to demonstrate what Mr. Jacobs sounded like on his trumpet and his mouthpiece. Very quickly a pattern begins to form, not of just playing a note but of sounding a certain way. This is important to the human brain. In other words, the brain of the artist is like a storyteller, like that of an actor; you have a message for somebody in the audience. And the brain should not be tremendously involved in the piece of brass; it should be tremendously involved in the music you're going to produce with it. That means you have to develop a conditioning in the player.

I prefer that the young player is conditioned in the phenomena of sounds, phrases, emotions, and rhythms of music. I want him to be expert in music, not in trumpet, not in tuba. I want him to be expert in the sounds of the instruments. This little psychological twist is very important because so many of the people want to learn the instrument in order to play the music. I want them to learn the music and while they're learning the music, they're learning their instrument. I put the emphasis on very easy music that can be played without technical knowledge, but I want the heavy questions to be what the audience is going to hear from this instrument, not the methodology of producing it. You have to do this

132

because of the enormous power of the human brain to acquire information. With young students, there is a tremendous ability to learn. In other words, the ability of the brain to gather information is far greater than to impart information.

I'll close this simply by stating that as far as I'm concerned, in a pedagogical sense, I would like the emphasis to be on a non-technical way of teaching so that the teacher may understand psychophysiology and the human function; but as a player, become a storyteller himself. In guiding others, I would like teachers to focus primarily on the music. That includes qualities of tone, emotions, rhythms, excitement, and all the things that are involved in our particular art form.

Lecture given by Arnold Jacobs at the Second International Brass Congress, Indiana University, June 6, 1984

The following are excerpts from the text of a lecture presented by Arnold Jacobs during the Second International Brass Congress at Indiana University on June 6, 1984. Immediately preceding the lecture the Second International Brass Congress Award was presented to Arnold Jacobs by Philip Farkas.

As with the preceeding lecture, minor changes have been made to adapt Jacobs' words to the medium of print. The cuts made delete repeated information and visual demonstrations.

I want to thank all of you so much and also my good friends Philip [Farkas] and Dee Stewart, who studied with me many years ago, for this honor that you're bestowing upon me. I appreciate it so much, and I feel very fortunate to be here to receive this. I have had two serious illnesses, and in the last three weeks I have received nothing but the most excellent news. In other words, I expect to be talking to people for quite some years to come. I had a cancerous condition develop about two years ago and just recently I had some tests; they found no trace of it. I wanted to have a champagne celebration in my hospital room, but the doctors and nurses, while they were all for it, just wouldn't allow it. It was right after surgery, but the news was so good and I felt so good about it that I'm still celebrating.

As long as I was invited here, I would like to discuss a few things about the aspects of playing a musical instrument, be it in orchestral or solo work. But I prefer to talk about the people who play these instruments, because I think so many answers lie in the study of human beings and how they apply themselves to various functions in life, whether it's athletics, dancing, or other uses of the body. To do this, we have to go into sort of a study of analogous situations.

If you study machine systems or the structure of an automobile, you find an enormously complex mechanism that is put together by people in the manufacturing business. They put together nuts and bolts and pistons and all sorts of parts that are very complex.

But when they're through assembling the car, they always put in a control panel in the driver's compartment, so the driver can communicate to extremely complex machinery through simple controls. This leaves the driver free to cope with the phenomenon of transportation through traffic and as a rule he doesn't have to worry about what's going on under the hood. You press the gas pedal to go faster or reduce it by giving it less gas, step on the brakes to stop, steer left, steer right, but your brain is free to cope with the phenomenon of the external environment in relation to your car. The communication to the parts are simple; what's under the hood is complex.

The human body is the most complex machine on this planet. We have physicians who study for much of their lives to understand the workings of the human body because we are enormously complex. The one thing we cannot do is work with our human body as though we were the mechanic. You have 659 muscles in the human body, 654 paired as antagonists to each other; there is some variation on these thoughts depending on who the researchers are, but this is the basic information. There are 654 muscles to maneuver the skeletal structures, to permit you to take a glass of water, drink it, and do the things we just don't think about.

If we attached equipment on the musculatures of the body, we would find that lifting this glass involves enormously complex contractions coming from various parts of our anatomy so that I don't fall over because of gravitational changes. Because the weight of the arm is heavier than the scapular in the back, little muscles have to fasten it down. Hundreds of muscular changes occur, maybe even thousands, simply by picking this glass up. To try to understand this and maneuver your body by controlling your muscles; it's just foolish. In my studies I have learned that it is important to recognize that we have levels of the brain that do different things. The level of the brain that allows us to learn or impart knowledge is also the region that allows us to cope with life around us, not life within us. What I want to bring out is that you have to have the thinking part of the brain programmed for the study of music.

Music is sound, a phenomenon of sound. The sensors that are going to hear it have to do with the audio aspects of our art form, and we will use vision to see who's playing. I can almost tell when I look at students and watch them play who they study with. Without realizing it students pick up the characteristics of the teacher. Vincent Cichowicz was a student of mine many years ago. He teaches trumpet at Northwestern University. I can watch his students and know without asking who they study with. I know by what they look like, the way they hold their horns, the way they approach the aspect of playing, and of course, by what they sound like. I'm sure students who study with me pick up certain characteristics of mine. The sense of sight is one of our extremely powerful learning tools. We learn so much through vision. We learn through sound and through touch, the tactile sense.

So our brains must take care of the internal environment. This is done by the study of emotion, by the body's needs for food and respiration, the body's basic needs. We are involved in that, but we are not involved in how the phenomenon of musculature coordination is achieved, how the many fiber groups contract to swing a golf club, how they're coordinated, what fibers are innervated, and what ones are not. If we study products rather than methods, it is extremely simple to function. When I pick up this glass, this is a product. I have to bring it to my lips. If I have to search around and find my lips, a neurological examination would probably find that there's been a disruption in the brain and possibly in the nerves that must signal the muscles, or in the muscles themselves. But if I can bring it directly to my lips, I have functioned normally and I don't have to think of the various muscles involved.

[Jacobs then picked up his mouthpiece to demonstrate buzzing.]

In playing I want the attention to go off the embouchure and onto the fact that the lips must vibrate. They must vibrate because the horn picks up vibration and amplifies it as sound waves. Air going through the instrument is not amplified; you'll hear a noise of air, but you don't play by air, you play by sound. If we could use electronic stimulation to vibrate the lips, we wouldn't need air, but we would need vibration. Well, unfortunately, we can't use electronics to vibrate our embouchures, so we must use breath. I'm noted as a teacher because I've developed quite a reputation as a specialist in the use of respiratory function in wind instrument playing and singing. I like to put the subject into perspective. It's an important subject, but it has to do with being a live human being, not just being a musician. The body really knows nothing about trumpet playing or tuba playing or French horn playing. These are additives; these are things that we add to our development. Our basic structure is simply to survive on this planet, and we make use of some of these factors in order to buzz that mouth-piece, play a trumpet, or sing, or whatever. I suspect it was not in the original design, but occurred as a developmental aspect as people continued to survive on this planet.

You can't really study the phenomenon of respiration without studying childbirth, strange as it seems. Today, there's more recognition of this in natural childbirth and what they do with the breath to help. The respiratory musculature is involved in three phenomena of life; two have nothing to do with the direct aspect of gas exchange in respiration, but they do have to do with the supportive aspect of respiration to downward contracting diaphragms. In other words, increasing intra-abdominal or pelvic pressures. In childbirth, as well as defecation, there is a bearing down where a person takes a breath. You watch a small child take a breath and the face will turn red when they have to eliminate feces. You can see the blood pressure going up; they have what is called the Valsalva maneuver, the closing of the larynx which acts as a stopper to the respiratory system.

In the meantime, after having taken a breath, the rib cage will contract and help increase air pressure to push down on the downward contracting diaphragm. If the pressure has to be very great, the person will show distress signs very quickly; if you palpate or touch the internal structure of the individual, you'll feel great contraction states in the abdominal region. When these are in isometric contraction of this type, you are getting the potential of vast increases in intra-abdominal pressure. It is difficult to use your air in quantity at that time. You could open the larynx and use it under great pressure in small quantity because the muscles are in contraction against each other. As a result, they cannot move freely in large maneuvers. This maneuver works fine in powerful blowing of small quantities, which you would have on piccolo trumpet or oboe, because you don't need many liters of air per minute flow rate. Air can be put under intensive pressure through this particular maneuver, which in life belongs to the pelvic pressure syndrome.

Another maneuver which we all have occurs in certain athletic procedures or combat situations where you harden the frontal abdominal wall. Muscles that are not in use will have muscle tone. A small number of fibers in each muscle group will be innervated, but you're not doing anything. If out of, say, 1,000 fibers, if 15 or 20 are innervated just to have muscle tone, this is a healthy situation. What I would not want to feel is a powerful contraction as I palpate the abdominal region. That would mean that there are large muscle groups that are fighting each other, which would bring about fatigue states. This will desensitize the region in terms of some of the sensitive functions that we need.

[Using volunteers, Jacobs gave a visual demonstration showing the strength of the abdominal muscles.]

In music, there's a conditioning that the young player must go through right from his first lesson. We have to have scales; we have to have interval studies; we have to have studies of music. We can take a young mind, and we have the ability to stimulate that mind with music. This is what you do with a young player who wants to play.

I can give you some illustrations of this. This has to do with the Suzuki method, and I think I can best express it by talking a little about myself. I was born in Philadelphia a long time ago; I'll be 69 on June the 11th, so that's many years ago. I was born into a musical family, but in those days we didn't have radio. The radio was just coming in; they used copper wire wrapped around an oatmeal box, and they would have a little crystal and ear phones. If you were lucky enough, there was a radio station somewhere close by and you would hear something. We didn't have the advantage of hearing a great deal of music on radio or being exposed to things you would normally be exposed to on television. We had to make our own entertainment at home.

My mother was a professional pianist, a very fine one. When I was about six months old, we left Philadelphia and moved to Long Beach, California, so I grew up in California. In the years when I first became interested in music, we lived in a little town called Willow Brook on the edge of the California desert. It was a town of 400 or so, and it was great. My mother used to play hours and hours a day and for entertainment, we would sing. My brain was being flooded with sound. I was not only the recipient of sound, but I also had to produce sound because I was using song, which meant the sensors were gathering information and the brain was learning to receive and recognize sound quite well. I was also using the psychomotor phenomenon of motor activity to influence others through sound. When I was 10 or 11, I wanted a bugle, so my parents bought me one, and my mother would play bugle calls on the piano. By listening to them I learned to play the bugle by

138

ear. I think you could literally find the Suzuki aspect here. A young child learns to produce sounds. First hearing them, then producing them. So the phenomenon of imitation is one of our very powerful learning tools.

The sense of sight is also extremely powerful. Imitation of sounds and sight and both senses reinforcing each other is one of the ways to go. In my own development, I worked with my mother. I remember becoming a boy scout, they put me in uniform before I was old enough to be a scout, but they needed a bugler. So I was a success on the bugle. I remember going down these dark street at night playing my bugle (much to the horror of the neighbors), and making a real pest out of myself; but I won a silverplated bugle in scout competition when I was quite young. Then I asked my father if I could have a trumpet. He bought me a trumpet, but no instruction book, just a trumpet. Naturally, I was able to play the seven positions of the valves and my mother would play, and I would figure out fingerings and write them down because we didn't have the instruction book. I often think of that and my career after that.

That really was quite a good thing to do because again, it was developing in terms of functional ability not only in the receiving of sound but in influencing the external environment by producing music. What you get through sensors and what you impart through motor systems are quite different. So the encouragement of the child in the Suzuki method, the constant repetition, which is a conditioning factor for the brain and the learning process, and the ability of muscles to respond to these thoughts are being illustrated in a beautiful way.

When I have students who come to me, one of the first things I ask them to do is to play something by memory. If they can't think of anything, I say I don't care what it is. It could be "My Country 'Tis of Thee" or "The Star Spangled Banner", or it could be some rock or dixieland tune. I don't care what it is, because I want them to play something they have conceived and I want them to teach me. It's a psychomotor function; you influence the external environment through motor systems. Our excellence in learning is through sensors. But how excellent are we at imparting knowledge? This has to be done; you influence the external environment no matter what you do through motor systems. If I move this microphone, I'm doing it through motor systems. When I talk to you, I'm using motor systems. You're listening to me and you're using sensors. Those of us who teach and those of us who are going to be

139

in the art form of music have to make sure we don't get so involved with spelling "m-u-s-i-c" or so involved in talking about music that we don't get involved in playing music.

When you put up a sheet of music, you learn what's on the page. Just like an actor on the stage, you think about what it will sound like to anybody who is listening to the music. As soon as you start interpreting, there is an immediate change from the act of learning. It's far different when you impart knowledge to somebody else, than when you learn it for yourself. Those of you who play should always have somebody in your imagination who you're playing for. I watch people in my studio when they're learning something; they're looking and reading the music like it was a textbook.

The learning power a youngster has and how he acquires information that comes through sensors to the brain is tremendous. But how excellent are they at influencing the external environment by imparting information? This is what we have to realize as teachers. There has to be a deliberate effort on all our parts to begin to communicate to others with our music, to become a storyteller of sound, phrase, and emotion, and all of the phenomena we use in our art form. We can't take this for granted. Admittedly, there will be students who come to me who have this talent and with them we don't have to worry much about it. Then there comes another boy who may be an "A" student in physics, but he doesn't tell a story when he plays; he's thinking of the phenomenon of measurement. That doesn't mean he's without talent; it simply means that this young man has to be made to realize that there are emotions to music and that the tools of it will be emotions in the brain. We have to deal with specific phenomena of patterns of response and tissue, which have become conditioned reflexes. That means we must provide stimulus. There is no such thing as a response without a stimulus. The problems we have actually go further and further into the brain; if we want to find embouchure, we have to develop it by playing music. We have to do it by what we do with music.

In the development of tissue, we have what you call hypertrophy of fibers where they enlarge and strengthen; this comes in the act of playing. It is not learned by instructions on how to use your lip. In the elementary stages, the lip has not gone through hypertrophy. These fibers are not going to be able to have much range; they won't have much ability to change and all things will be crude. In the study of physical skills, you always find that you start

140

out with crudeness and develop skills. It's the same with any muscle group, whether it's golf or whether it's playing the tuba. We have to make sure a student is allowed to develop and we do this by encouraging excellence in conceptual thought and permitting mistakes. It's no big deal if somebody makes a mistake, but what were the thoughts when they were making the mistake? I encourage a tremendous effort for the art form, then I want the disciplines of practice. I believe in that thoroughly because of the conditioning factors involved. To me, playing a scale is like a prize fighter punching a bag and jumping rope, but I want that scale to be more than punching a bag or jumping rope; I want it to be a cadenza from Mozart, or I want it to be part of a good jazz figure. We have to put it right back into the art form of music.

What I'm doing is working with a human being who plays a musical instrument. He has a piece of brass in hand; that brass has no brains so we cannot limit ourselves to the potential of the brass and say, well, I'm learning to play a trumpet, or I'm learning to play a horn or a tuba. You're learning to play music with these instruments, so the dominance is the sound that comes out of the bell; it's like circuitry in electronics. You conceive the sound you want either by imitating the teacher, a colleague, or a record, but you conceive and then you listen to find out if you sound like what you want to sound like. The important thing is not what you sound like, it's what you want to sound like. 85 percent of the intellectual approach to music is conceptual thought, 15 percent is the readout that comes out of the bell of the horn, which is sensory. In other words, what do you sound like to me? I have people who come to me and only listen to themselves; they're not conceiving. The horn has no brains; it can't really give you anything, you have to give it to the horn.

[The discussion then turned to tone production. This information can be found in the other Jacobs lecture from the International Brass Congress, also included in this book.]

I consider mouthpiece work to be very important when you're working with remedial cases. Or if a student wants to check himself out, playing on the mouthpiece removes the acoustical device. It is wonderful to sing a part and play it on the mouthpiece. By removing the horn, you have removed one of the powerful forms of stimulus that develops over the years. A person picks up the horn, puts his hand in position, notes pop into the head; there are all sorts of stimuli involved with the instrument. If there's something wrong and we want to introduce change, I immediately remove the trumpet but have the student play on the mouthpiece so that he is forced into recall and mentalization. Removing the instrument forces him into the recall and we can immediately concentrate more on the musical factor. All of the tissues involved in playing the instrument are still involved in playing the mouthpiece, every one except the right hand or the left hand, depending on the instrument. But making music is involved in brain and reflex responses that condition response in the embouchure to thought.

If you think of vocal cord activity, you'll find that the lips actually become the vocal cords of the brass instrument. These are complicated thoughts, but this is the basic aspect of playing a brass instrument. You're very close to singing because the sound sent out of a brass instrument only has the ability to resonate according to its acoustical laws. It does not have the ability to provide you with the pitch when you just blow, like in some of the woodwinds. So the brass instrument is close to singing, and I think the brass player should mentally consider himself close to the singer, not in a technical sense of physical application, but in the musical sense of vocal cord activity in the embouchure and expressing thoughts with it.

There is great benefit to making music with the lips alone, but I would strongly suggest the use of a rim of the mouthpiece. When I was young I realized that playing on the mouthpiece alone is a fabulous tool which I now use a great deal in teaching, when I want to focus on the mentalization. I have to create strangeness. If we want to change a situation of response, we don't do it by the study of the muscle that's responding, we do it by the study of the stimuli that's causing the muscle to respond. We must change the stimulus in order to change the pattern of response. To do that you introduce strangeness or you can't create change.

Now let me have some questions. We have a few moments for it. Yes.

Besides breathing in large volumes of air and trying to relax, what helps us to breathe freely and steadily?

Again, the key to inhalation is to go back to the study of the human being and not to the study of repiratory functions. The goal is to find the ability to inhale based on suction with minimal friction. In other words, suction is the clue for the diaphragmatic descent. If you were to fluoroscope a person taking a breath based on the free movements of air, you would find that this function is linked to a center of the brain that has wonderful efficiency for ordering a large volume of air into the mouth. You're not guiding it based on the physical phenomenon of what we know according to Boyle's law to be the enlargement phenomenon of the thorax; you're going through the psychological attitudes of respiration. Yawning without opening your mouth wide is a wonderful tool. Very little strength is involved. What we don't want is resistances.

[Jacobs then demonstrated a lung capacity measurement device.]

We need to have the ability to move large quantities of air in and out of the mouth. If it goes in and out of the mouth, there is no way to have a large quantity of air go in the mouth without it going to the right places. It will automatically be there because you can't take a large quantity without the proper inflation of the lungs, and the same thing is true when moving it out. I don't want the psychology of respiration to involve the physical apparatus, but how much air you take in and how much air you blow out.

[Jacobs next had a volunteer try the lung capacity measurement device, and the session came to a close.]

Arnold Jacobs at Ravinia, taken by Jerry Sirucek

Arnold Jacobs:
A biography based on the Chicago Symphony file

Arnold Jacobs, principal tuba of the Chicago Symphony Orchestra, was born in Philadelphia, but was raised in California. The product of a musical family, he credits his mother, a keyboard artist, for his initial inspiration in music, and spent a good part of his youth progressing from bugle to trumpet to trombone and finally to tuba. He entered Philadelphia's Curtis Institute of Music as a 15-year-old on a scholarship and continued to major in tuba.

After his graduation from Curtis in 1936, he played two seasons in the Indianapolis Symphony under Fabien Sevitzky. From 1939 until 1944 he was tuba in the Pittsburgh Symphony under Fritz Reiner. In 1941 Mr. Jacobs toured the country with Leopold Stokowski and the All-American Youth Orchestra. He joined the Chicago Symphony in 1944, and during the spring of 1949 he took a temporary leave from the Orchestra to tour England and Scotland with the Philadelphia Orchestra. In June, 1962, he had the honor of being the first tuba player invited to play at the Casals Festival in Puerto Rico.

Mr. Jacobs is a member of the Chicago Symphony Brass Quintet and recently retired after many years of teaching tuba at the Northwestern University School of Music. In addition to his students around the world, he also teaches and coaches for the Civic Orchestra of Chicago.

Mr. Jacobs has given lectures and clinics throughout the United States and Canada, and is widely known as a teacher of brass instruments, specializing in respiratory and motivational applications for both brass and wind instrument playing and voice.

During the Orchestra's 1977 and 1985 Japanese tours, Mr. Jacobs was a clinician for the Yamaha Band Instrument Company in Tokyo. In January, 1978, he was invited to lecture at Michael Reese Hospital on the use of playing wind instruments in the therapeutic treatment of asthma in children. In 1984, the Second International Brass Congress presented its highest award to Arnold Jacobs.

Mr. Jacobs was given an honorary Doctor of Music degree from VanderCook College in 1986.

Mr. Jacobs can be heard as the soloist on the Chicago Symphony's recording of Vaughan Williams' Tuba Concerto, conducted by Daniel Barenboim and released by Deutsche Grammophon.

Teaching in his studio

Rich Mays

Arnold Jacobs
The Legacy of a Master

Begun with the idea of paying tribute to the great "Doctor of Brass Playing" and of documenting the pedagogical principles of the renowned teacher, *Arnold Jacobs: The Legacy of a Master* will be of interest to those who already know Arnold Jacobs and to those who will come to know him through these pages. Compiled and edited by Dee Stewart, a Jacobs student and a teacher at Indiana University, the book is made up of recollections of Arnold Jacobs' students and colleagues, many of whom now play in orchestras around the country.

Anecdotes from lessons and performances, pedagogical ideas (including some of the breathing techniques Jacobs is famous for) and stories of lasting friendships are all in these reminiscences. Contributors range from one of his earliest students, who recalls that his lessons cost $1 for an undetermined length, to more recent students.

As Dee Stewart says, "Musicians rarely have the opportunity to appreciate the works of a great pedagogue. Teachers frequently theorize on their methods in books and articles, but the products of their teaching, the successful students, are often less obvious...the contributors to this collection feel that the training and association they have had with Mr. Jacobs dramatically shaped their lives and careers."